SpringerBriefs in Computer Science

T0184452

For further volumes:
http://www.springer.com/series/10028

José Viterbo · Markus Endler

Decentralized Reasoning
in Ambient Intelligence

 Springer

José Viterbo
Department of Computer Science
Universidade Federal Fluminense (UFF)
Niterói, RJ
Brazil

Markus Endler
Department of Informatics
Pontifícia Universidade Católica do
   Rio de Janeiro (PUC-Rio)
Rio de Janeiro, RJ
Brazil

ISSN 2191-5768   ISSN 2191-5776   (electronic)
ISBN 978-1-4471-4167-9   ISBN 978-1-4471-4168-6   (eBook)
DOI 10.1007/978-1-4471-4168-6
Springer London Heidelberg New York Dordrecht

Library of Congress Control Number: 2012938143

Printed on acid-free paper

Springer is part of Springer Science+Business Media (www.springer.com)

Contents

Acronyms

ABox	Assertional box
AmI	Ambient Intelligence
API	Application programming interface
CMS	Context model service
ConfComp	Conference companion application
ConfOrg	Conference organizer application
DL	Description logics
DRS	Decentralized reasoning service
DRS/A	Ambient decentralized reasoning service
DRS/D	Device decentralized reasoning service
FOL	First order logic
HTTP	Hypertext transfer protocol
IP	Internet protocol
J2ME	Java 2 Platform, Micro edition
MoCA	Mobile collaboration architecture
OWL	Web ontology language
P2P	Peer-to-peer
RDF	Resource description framework
SWRL	Semantic Web Rule Language
TBox	Terminological box

Chapter 1
Introduction

Abstract In this chapter we clarify the motivations and purpose of this work. Initially, in the next section, in order to explain what instigated our research, we present a brief overview about Ambient Intelligence, the research area in which lies the object of this work. In Sect. 1.2 we discuss, in detail, the problem addressed in this work and its main characteristics, setting the scope of the proposed approach. In Sect. 1.3 we clearly define the goal we pursued during our research work. Finally, in Sect. 1.4 we describe the general organization of this work.

Keywords Ambient Intelligence · Ubiquitous computing · Context-awareness · Rule-based reasoning · Decentralized reasoning · Cooperative reasoning

1.1 Overview

Ubiquitous computing features the seamless integration of computer systems into the everyday lives of users to provide information and functionalities anytime and anywhere [33]. It involves the interaction of diverse computational devices aiming at providing services to support users in a transparent and continuous way. For this purpose, ubiquitous computing environments encompass different kinds of sensors and mobile devices (e.g., PDAs, notebooks, smartphones), interconnected through a combination of several wireless network technologies.

Compared to traditional distributed systems, ubiquitous computing systems are characterized by an increased dynamism and heterogeneity of devices, applications and services [29]. The underlying ubiquitous computing infrastructures are more complex and bring into the foreground issues such as user mobility, device disconnections, join and leave of devices, heterogeneous networks, as well as the need to integrate the physical environment with the computing infrastructure [18]. A software infrastructure to support the execution of ubiquitous applications has to be flexible and reactive to deal with the unpredictable, heterogeneous and dynamic

J. Viterbo and M. Endler, *Decentralized Reasoning in Ambient Intelligence*,
SpringerBriefs in Computer Science, DOI: 10.1007/978-1-4471-4168-6_1,
© The Author(s) 2012

nature of the computing environments encountered when users move around different locations [21].

In ubiquitous computing environments, a large number of autonomous software entities, i.e., ubiquitous applications and services, work together to transform physical spaces into smart and interactive environments [23]. In such scenarios, new issues are beginning to arise, such as how to enable users to continuously perform their computational tasks while moving through different locations [30], how to enable users to cooperate while located in different places [22], or how to promote ad-hoc cooperation in situations when a group of users sharing common interests unexpectedly meet at the same location and need to engage in collective activities [7].

The approaches and technologies for supporting these new ways of working are still under investigation. Nevertheless, a particularly interesting trend in ubiquitous computing is exploring the Ambient Intelligence (AmI) paradigm, a multidisciplinary approach that aims at the integration of innovative sensing, communication and actuation technologies to create computer-mediated environments that support user activities through specific services of the environment, provisioned with minimal user intervention [31].

A prominent example of an environment enriched with AmI is a "smart home", a house equipped to bring advanced services to its users [3]. In such an environment, several domestic artifacts and items can be enriched with sensors to gather information about their use and in some cases even to act independently without human intervention [11]. For instance, door locks in a smart home could be capable of identifying persons and permitting hands-free opening, which could be a useful functionality for elderly, children and disabled people, as well as parents entering the home with both hands occupied with carrying shopping bags and guiding several children along [15].

Another class of applications for AmI focuses on providing health monitoring and support to individuals with cognitive or physical impairments, aiming at helping these people to live independently by improving their access to a wide range of services and facilities [24]. For example, in the case of people at an early stage of senile dementia—the most frequent case being elderly people suffering from Alzheimer's disease—such a system could be tailored to ensure appropriate care at critical times by monitoring activities, diagnosing risk situations—such as a stroke or heart attack—and advising a carer or doctor in case of need [4].

There has been also a lot of significant work on the use of AmI technologies for facilitating interaction in academic environments, such as universities [26, 27], research centers [12], conference facilities [25, 9], i.e., environments where researchers, teachers and students gather to engage in learning activities or participate in technical meetings and presentations. In such a scenario, for instance, after detecting that all listed key participants in a pre-arranged meeting have already arrived in the respective room, an AmI service could dim the lights, stop the background music and turn on the projector in that room [10].

Essentially, an AmI system should be aware of the presence of people in the geographical space, perceive their needs and be able to autonomously personalize and make available services to help users to perform their tasks [14]. For that reason, as a fundamental requirement, AmI applications must be capable of automatically responding to dynamic changes in the environment—such as a person entering or leaving a room, a steep increase in the temperature indicated by a sensor or a new device connecting to the local network, etc—with none or minimal human interference. Hence, applications executing in AmI systems are intrinsically context-aware, i.e., they have to strongly rely on context data collected from sensors embedded into the environment and in the user's devices to trigger adaptations at different levels, such as in the wireless communication links, middleware and application services, or the user interfaces.

AmI requires middleware support for software development—and deployment— capable of integrating large quantities of different devices and sensors and building a programmable and auto-configurable infrastructure [23]. Several projects, e.g., Gaia [25], CoBrA [9], CHIL [28], etc., have developed prototypes of such environments, usually focusing on specific use cases, user tasks or application domains. In general, these middleware systems provide not only services to store, distribute and process context data collected from different sources, but also services for reasoning about context information, which may be based on logical inference using some type of derivation rule mechanism, e.g., first-order logic, descriptive logic, case-based reasoning or fuzzy logic, or other specialized techniques, such as neural networks, Bayesian networks, etc [17].

In AmI systems, as in most ubiquitous systems, reasoning is necessary for several purposes. First, it is required for dealing with the intrinsic imperfection and uncertainty of context data [16]. In this way, reasoning allows the detection of possible errors, to estimate missing values, to determine the quality, precision and validity of the context information. It could be used, for instance, for resolving conflicts when different positioning methods inform different locations for a same entity. For example, when a user forgets his GPS-enabled smart phone in a meeting room and logs in to his office's workstation [8], both pieces of information are provided to the middleware. Second, reasoning may also be used for determining higher-level context information, i.e., inferring new, implicit pieces of context information derived from raw context data. For example, reasoning could be used to determine that a seminar has started based on information about the location of a speaker in a conference room and on the volume of noise proceeding from the pulpit area [29]. Third, reasoning is fundamental for triggering actions or adaptations according to specific situations that may be meaningful and relevant to some applications [13]. For example, reasoning could be used to identify that a user is busy when he is in a meeting room with at least one other colleague, his coffee cup and at least one of his colleagues' coffee cups are co-located in the same room and are warm [19].

In most cases, context reasoning in AmI systems is very complex due to the dynamic, imprecise and ambiguous nature of context information and the need to process large volumes of data collected from a large number of context providers. This complexity is increased by the fact that in some conditions reasoning needs to be performed in a decentralized way involving several entities of the system [5]. Decentralization takes the form of physical distribution of computing and sensor devices, context providers and consumers, entities responsible for brokering and reasoning, and ambient services, applications and users that may potentially interact.

1.2 Problem Setting

In the design of ubiquitous applications, the *situation abstraction* is regarded as a powerful feature [13]. Situations are defined as particular combinations of aggregated context data [1], which are relevant for triggering actions or adaptations in applications or services [34]. Rules provide a formal model—based on some type of logic—for describing these situations, which hence may be identified by reasoning operations [2]. Moreover, by using rules the application developer can define the relevant situations apart from the application code, achieving great flexibility: he may easily modify previously defined rules to adapt applications to different domains or reuse available rules to describe new situations. Therefore, rule-based inference mechanisms are a fundamental requirement for middleware systems that support the development and deployment of AmI services and applications.

Most middleware systems adopt a centralized approach for their reasoning mechanisms. For example, CoBrA [9], CHIL [28] and Semantic Space [32] are middleware systems that aim at the deployment of small scale smart rooms, where a central server collects all context data available in such ambients—provided either by sensors or user's devices—and performs all reasoning operations. In AmI environments, however, these reasoning operations may need to evaluate context data collected from distributed sources and stored in different devices, as usually not all context data is readily available to the reasoners within a ubiquitous system. For reasons ranging from privacy to performance issues, a fully distributed reasoning scheme is regarded as a necessity [6]. In fact, distributed reasoners that work with small partitions of large context data sets, such as in OWL-SF [20], may have a better performance locally. Nevertheless, if the result of the inference depends on context data distributed among different partitions, the communication overhead necessary to produce a combined result may be excessively high, reducing the scalability of the system.

In our work, we model an AmI system with the understanding that there are two main interacting tiers in the reasoning process: the *user side*, comprised by the user's devices and client applications, and the *ambient side*, represented by the ambient infrastructure and its services, each managing different context information. We assume that, for reasons ranging from privacy to performance, neither side is prone to disclose its context information, and as such, neither side has access to all context data. In this case, context reasoning has to be executed in a decentralized way, involving reasoners at both sides, performing what we define as "cooperative reasoning".

1.3 Goals

This work proposes a decentralized reasoning approach for performing rule-based reasoning about context data targeting AmI systems, according to the characteristics of our model, i.e., considering that there are two main interacting parties in the reasoning process: the *user side* and the *ambient side*. We assume that each side has access to different context information, which is not shared with the other side. As such, we propose a novel *cooperative reasoning* approach, in which two entities cooperate to perform a split inference of facts involving data distributed between the two tiers. To show the feasibility of this approach, we designed, implemented and evaluated a middleware service supporting decentralized reasoning based on the cooperation of reasoning services located on each side. The service is expected to be scalable to support a large number of clients, robust to deal with message failures, portable for mobile devices and expressive to represent a wide variety of rules.

As such, the main contributions of this work are the following:

- The identification of a trade-off between completely distributed reasoning systems and systems that are capable of evaluating complex rules with variables, offering greater expressiveness.
- The definition of a context model for AmI environments assuming that context data is distributed over two sides, the *user side*, represented by the users and their mobile devices, and the *ambient side*, represented by the fixed computational infrastructure and ambient services.
- The enumeration and discussion of a set of design strategies for a distributed reasoning service tailored for AmI environments that follow the model defined before.
- The formalization of the *cooperative reasoning* operation, in terms of a split inference of facts involving data distributed in two tiers.
- The definition of a complete process—comprising a strategy, a protocol and the corresponding algorithms—to perform the *cooperative reasoning*, i.e., in which two entities cooperate to perform decentralized rule-based reasoning.
- The implementation and evaluation of a prototype middleware service using KAON2 and MoCA's publish/subscribe service for performing cooperative rule-based reasoning.

It is important to emphasize that, despite the fact that some works have presented different approaches for distributed reasoning, our two-tier proposal for modeling context data in AmI environments—and the respective process for split inference of facts—are original contributions for this subject.

1.4 Organization

In the next chapter, we present an AmI scenario and explain the fundamental concepts involved in this work: Ambient Intelligence, context-awareness, ontology-based context model, context reasoning and rule-based reasoning, giving clear definitions about all these concepts and examples involving our scenario. In Chap. 3, we describe some research projects related to our topic, namely Gaia, OWL-SF, DRAGO, P2P-DR, and P2PIS, explaining how they tackle the distributed reasoning problem. In Chap. 4, we describe our approach for enabling decentralized reasoning, discussing the design strategies for implementing a service capable of executing the approach. In Chap. 5, we define a strategy, protocols and algorithms for decentralized reasoning. In Chap. 6, we explain our strategy by means of a case study. In Chap. 7, we present the Decentralized Reasoning Service (DRS), a prototype middleware service that implements the proposed approach, and a prototype application that exemplifies how this service may be used. In Chap. 8, we describe the functional and performance tests that were made on the Decentralized Reasoning Service (DRS) and evaluate the results. Finally, in Chap. 9, we discuss the contributions and limitations of our approach and suggest some topics for future work.

References

1. Anagnostopoulos, C.B., Hadjiefthymiades, S.: Enhancing situation-aware systems through imprecise reasoning. IEEE Trans. Mobile Comput. 7(10), 1153–1168 (2008)
2. Anagnostopoulos, C.B., Ntarladimas, Y., Hadjiefthymiades, S.: Situational computing: An innovative architecture with imprecise reasoning. J. Syst. Softw. 80(12), 1993–2014 (2007)
3. Augusto, J., McCullagh, P.: Ambient intelligence: concepts and applications. Comput. Sci. Inform. Syst. (ComSIS) 4(1), 1–26 (2007)
4. Augusto, J.C.: Ambient intelligence: the confluence of ubiquitous/pervasive computing and artificial intelligence. In: Schuster, A.J. (eds.) Intelligent Computing Everywhere, Chappter 11, pp. 213—234. Springer, London (2007)
5. Bikakis, A., Antoniou, G.: Distributed reasoning with conflicts in an ambient peer-to-peer setting. In: Bergmann, R., Althoff, K.D., Furbach, U., Schmid, K. (eds.) Proceedings of the Workshop Artificial Intelligence Methods for Ambient Intelligence at the European Conference on Ambient Intelligence (AmI'07), pp. 25–34 (2007)
6. Bikakis, A., Patkos, T., Antoniou, G., Plexousakis, D.: A survey of semantics-based approaches for context reasoning in ambient intelligence. In: Bergmann, R., Althoff, K.D., Furbach, U., Schmid, K. (eds.) Proceedings of the Workshop Artificial Intelligence Methods for Ambient Intelligence at the European Conference on Ambient Intelligence (AmI'07), pp. 15–24 (2007)
7. Bottazzi, D., Montanari, R., Toninelli, A.: Context-aware middleware for anytime, anywhere social networks. IEEE Intell. Syst. 22(5), 22–32 (2007)
8. Chen, H.: An Intelligent Broker Architecture for Pervasive Context-Aware Systems. Ph.D. thesis, University of Maryland, Baltimore (2004)
9. Chen, H., Finin, T., Joshi, A.: A context broker for building smart meeting rooms. In: Proceedings of the Knowledge Representation and Ontology for Autonomous Systems Symposium, pp. 53–60 (2004)
10. Chen, H., Finin, T., Joshi, A., Kagal, L., Chakraborty, F.: Intelligent agents meet the semantic web in smart spaces. IEEE Internet Comput. 8(6), 69–79 (2004)
11. Cook, D., Augusto, J., Jakkula, V.: Ambient intelligence: technologies, applications, and opportunities. Pervasive Mobile Comput. 5, 277–298 (2009)
12. Davies, N., Gellersen, H.W.: Beyond prototypes: challenges in deploying ubiquitous systems. IEEE Pervasive Comput. 1(1), 26–35 (2002)
13. Dey, A.: Understanding and using context. Pers. Ubiquit. Comput. 5(1), 4–7 (2001)
14. Ducatel, K., Bogdanowicz, M., Scapolo, F., Leijten, J., Burgelma, J.C.: Scenarios for Ambient Intelligence in 2010. Final report, IST Advisory Group (2001)

15. Friedewald, M., Costa, O., Punie, Y., Alahuhta, P., Heinonen, S.: Perspectives of ambient intelligence in the home environment. Telematics Inform. **22**, 221–238 (2005)
16. Henricksen, K., Indulska, J.: Modelling and using imperfect context information. In: Proceedings of Second IEEE Annual Conference on Pervasive Computing and Communications Workshops. IEEE Computer Society (2004)
17. Jie, S., ZhaoHui, W.: Context reasoning technologies in ubiquitous computing environment. In: Proceedings of Embedded and Ubiquitous Computing (EUC 2006), pp. 1027–1036 (2006)
18. Kindberg, T., Fox, A.: System software for ubiquitous computing. Pervasive Comput. Mag. (2002)
19. Loke, S.: On representing situations for context-aware pervasive computing: six ways to tell if you are in a meeting. In: Proceedings of the 4th Annual IEEE International Conference on Pervasive Computing and Communications Workshops (PERCOMW'06), p. 35. (2006)
20. Mrohs, B., Luther, M., Vaidya, R., Wagner, M., Steglich, S., Kellerer, W., Arbanowski, S.: OWL-SF—A distributed semantic service framework. In: Proceedings of Workshop on Context Awareness for Proactive Systems (CAPS), pp. 67–78. Helsinki, Finland (2005)
21. Murphy, A., Picco, G., Roman, G.C.: Lime: a middleware for physical and logical mobility. In: Proceedings of the 21st International Conference in Distributed Computing Systems, pp. 524–533. IEEE Computer Society, Los Alamitos, CA, USA (2001)
22. Nijholt, A., Rienks, R., Zwiers, J., Reidsma, D.: Online and off-line visualization of meeting information and meeting support. Vis. Comput. **22**(12), 965–976 (2006)
23. Ranganathan, A., Campbell, R.: A middleware for context-aware agents in ubiquitous computing environments. Lecture Notes Comput. Sci. **2672**, 143–161 (2003)
24. Riva, G.: Ambient intelligence in health care. CyberPsychology Behav. **6**(3), 295–300 (2003)
25. Román, M., Hess, C., Cerqueira, R., Ranganathan, A., Campbell, R., Nahrstedt, K.: A middleware infrastructure for active spaces. IEEE Pervasive Comput. **1**(4), 74–83 (2002)
26. Sadeh, N., Gandon, F., Kwon, O.: Ambient intelligence: the mycampus experience. Technical Report CMU-ISRI-05-123, School of Computer Science, Carnegie Mellon Univerity, Pittsburgh, USA (2005)
27. Seghrouchni, A., Breitman, K., Sabouret, N., Endler, M., Charif, Y., Briot, J.P.: Ambient intelligence applications: introducing the Campus framework. In: Ferré, S., Rudolph, S. (eds.) Proceedings of the 13th IEEE International Conference on Engineering of Complex Computer Systems (ICECCS'08), pp. 165–174. Belfast, Northern Ireland (2008)
28. Soldatos, J., Dimakis, N., Stamatis, K., Polymenakos, L.: A breadboard architecture for pervasive context-aware services in smart spaces: middleware components and prototype applications. Pers. Ubiquit. Comput. J. **11**(3), 193–212 (2007). doi: 10.1007/s00779-006-0102-7
29. Soldatos, J., Pandis, I., Stamatis, K., Polymenakos, L., Crowley, J.: Agent based middleware infrastructure for autonomous context-aware ubiquitous computing services. Comput. Commun. Special Issue: Emerging Middleware for Next Generation Networks **30**(3), 577–591 (2007)
30. Sousa, J.P., Garlan, D.: Aura: An architectural framework for user mobility in ubiquitous computing environments. In: Proceedings of the 3rd IEEE/IFIP Conference on Software Architecture (WICSA 3), pp. 29–43. Kluwer Academic Publishers, Springer (2002)
31. Viterbo, J., Mazuel, L., Charif, Y., Endler, M., Sabouret, N., Breitman, K., Seghrouchni, A., Briot, J.P.: Ambient intelligence: management of distributed and heterogeneous context knowledge. In: Dargie, W. (eds.) Context-Aware Computing and Self-Managing Systems, Chapter. 4, pp. 79–128. Edited by Waltenegus Dargie. CRC/Francis and Taylor, New York, USA (2009)
32. Wang, X., Dong, J., Chin, C., Hettiarachchi, S., Zhang, D.: Semantic Space: An Infrastructure for Smart Spaces. Pervasive Comput. **3**(3), 32–39 (2004)
33. Weiser, M.: The computer for the twenty-first century. Sci. Am. **265**(3), 94–104 (1991)
34. Yau, S.S., Huang, D., Gong, H., Seth, S.: Development and runtime support for situation-aware application software in ubiquitous computing environments. In: Proceedings of the 28th Annual International Computer Software and Applications Conference (COMPSAC'04), pp. 452–457. Hong Kong, China (2004)

Chapter 2
Fundamental Concepts

Abstract In this chapter we present the main concepts necessary to comprehend this work. In the first section, we describe our motivating scenario, to which we will refer along this work, in order to exemplify and clarify our approach. In Sect. 2.2, we discuss commonly found characteristics of Ambient Intelligence. In Sect. 2.3 we discuss context-awareness, a fundamental aspect in AmI systems, and in Sect. 2.4 the use of ontologies as the basis of our context model. In Sect. 2.5 we discuss context reasoning in general and in Sect. 2.6 we focus on the rule-based reasoning approach. Finally, in the last section we argue about the interrelation among these topics.

Keywords Ambient Intelligence · Ubiquitous computing · Context-awareness · Context reasoning · Ontology · Context model · Context reasoning · Description logics · Rule-based reasoning

2.1 Scenario

As a typical scenario to exemplify our approach, we suppose a fictitious conference on Ubiquitous Computing (UbiConference) where several researchers from different universities and companies gather to present and discuss their recent work. We assume that the conference is divided in several technical sessions on subjects such as *Middleware*, *Ambient Intelligence*, etc, and panel sessions on detached subjects (e.g., *Privacy*). It also comprises workshops on specific subjects such as *Context Modeling and Reasoning*.

Professor Silva is a lecturer and researcher affiliated with the Informatics Department of PUC-Rio. He is also participating in the UbiConference in different roles: (a) he is a member of the Programme Committee (PC); (b) he will chair the *Middleware* session; (c) he will present a paper in the *Context Modeling and Reasoning* workshop; and, of course, (d) he will also be a general attendee of others sessions in the event.

J. Viterbo and M. Endler, *Decentralized Reasoning in Ambient Intelligence*,
SpringerBriefs in Computer Science, DOI: 10.1007/978-1-4471-4168-6_2,
© The Author(s) 2012

Let us assume that UbiConference takes place in a convention center with several meeting rooms equipped with some infrastructure to support the organizing committee and the attendees with ubiquitous services. A service called Conference Organizer (ConfOrg) is part of this infrastructure and aims at providing context-aware functionalities, such as notifying the participants about the beginning of presentations in which they may be interested, or alerting a PC member when the session chair is absent at the moment a session is about to start, for instance.

Previously, when registering at the event website, Silva downloaded and installed in his notebook the Conference Companion (ConfComp), an application provided by the organizers to help him not only with his agenda during the event, but also with identifying people with interests similar to his, thus stimulating the collaboration and social interactions with other researchers at the event. Let us further assume that ConfComp interacts with ConfOrg to provide the ubiquitous services mentioned before, tailored for Silva's preferences. For that reason, after installing ConfComp, Silva is asked to provide detailed information about his affiliation and subjects of interest. Besides that, Silva's notebook is configured to run an indoor positioning service (e.g., the MoCA's Location Inference Service [66]), capable of continuously determining in which room of the conference center he is located. However, Silva did not agree in disclosing any of his personal data—nor his location nor his preferences—to ConfOrg or to the others attendees.

When arriving at the UbiConference venue, the ConfOrg service detects that his notebook is connected to the local wireless network and automatically registers his presence at the conference. By then, Silva's ConfComp receives the updated schedule of the sessions that he selected to attend on that day. From this moment on, whenever he is outside the room of a session he wants to attend and it is about to start, ConfComp notifies him to hurry to the corresponding room. At the moments when there is no session of interest for Silva, ConfComp would suggest him to go to some presentation where a great part of the audience shares similar interests as him.

The described scenario comprises a series of applications and ambient services that exemplify just some of the possible uses for Ambient Intelligence technologies. In the following section we discuss this paradigm in further detail.

2.2 Ambient Intelligence

Ambient Intelligence (AmI), i.e., "intelligent" pervasive computing, builds on three recent key technologies [5]: Ubiquitous Computing [69], Ubiquitous Communication [55] and Intelligent User Interfaces [33]. Ubiquitous Computing is the integration of microprocessors into everyday objects like furniture, clothing, white goods, toys, even paint. Ubiquitous Communication enables these objects to communicate with each other and the user by means of *ad hoc* wireless networking. Intelligent User Interfaces enable the inhabitants of an AmI environment to control and interact with the environment in a natural (voice, gesture) and personalized way (preferences, context). In an AmI environment, massively distributed devices operate collectively, while embedded in the environment, using information and "intelligence" that is hold by the interconnected system [1].

AmI aims at making use of those entities in order to provide users with an environment that offers services when and if needed. As such, an AmI system has to be (a) unobtrusive, i.e., its services must not intrude on the user's consciousness unless he needs them; (b) personalized, i.e., it must be able to recognize the user and tailor its behavior to the user's needs; (c) adaptive, i.e., its behavior can change in response to a person's actions and environment's context; and (d) anticipatory, i.e., it must anticipate a person's desires and environment as much as possible without mediation [26].

An example of an environment enriched with AmI is a "smart home", where several domestic artifacts and items can be enriched with sensors to gather information about their use and in some cases even to act independently without human intervention [22]. This approach enables to achieve increased safety, comfort, or economy [7], e.g., by monitoring the activities of the user and providing assistance when a possibly harmful situation is developing, adjusting temperature automatically or turning off lights in an empty room, for instance.

AmI may also help impaired people to live independently, improving their access to a wide range of services and facilities [56]. Automated home care systems based on AmI technology aim at the prolongation of an independent life of assisted persons in their own homes, reducing the dependency on intensive personal care to a minimum and thereby increasing the quality of life for the affected group while substantially decreasing the costs for society [50].

Academic environments are also target area in which AmI systems—or prototypes—has particularly flourished. In places such as universities, research centers, conference rooms, etc., where lecturers and students engage in learning activities, researchers gather to run technical meetings, attendees join to listen to technical presentations, AmI technologies are useful to facilitate the interaction among all participants. A plethora of projects have presented solutions targeting these same spaces, such as Gaia [57], CoBrA [20], CHIL [60], Semantic Space [67], CASMAS [17] and others. This is also the flavor of our scenario, as described in Sect. 2.1.

One great challenge for AmI environments is how to adequately address the heterogeneity and dynamic nature of users, services and devices [48]. Other key issues in the development of AmI are context-awareness and context-based reasoning and how to identify and provide the most appropriate service for the user and his task [47]. The ultimate goal is to make the ambient services more *intelligent* and adaptive to the specific needs of their users, so that the users do not need to get involved in service discovery, usage and personalization.

Privacy is also a concern in AmI environments, as this technology is regarded as having the potential to create an invisible and comprehensive surveillance network. This is because AmI systems influence two important design parameters relating to privacy: the ability to monitor and the ability to search. Depending on what kind of motives one assumes for preserving privacy, ambient intelligence technology can become the driving factor for changing the scope and impact of privacy protection as it exists today, and creating substantially different social landscapes in the future [13].

Our Assumption

In this work, we assume that users carry one or more mobile devices enabled with positioning sensors. They move through different spaces and organizations, and each time they enter a physical environment enriched with AmI technology, applications executing on their devices autonomously interact with different ambient services, i.e., services executing on the ambient infrastructure. These services and applications personalize their functional behavior based on the context data available at the moment, but each has access to different parts of the overall context information (c.f. Sect. 2.1). Although privacy is a concern in AmI and a motivation to the study of distributed context scenarios, this subject will not be further discussed here.

2.3 Context-Awareness

Context-awareness is the ability of a system to sense the current environment and autonomously perform appropriate adaptations aiming at its optimal operation, customized behavior and facilitated user interaction [65]. When a user changes his context, it is desirable that the applications on his mobile devices be able to adapt to the new situation, and the environment be able to adapt its services according to the presence of the new user.

In AmI environments, more specifically, systems should be aware of the presence of persons in the geographical space, perceive their needs and autonomously make available and personalize services that help users to perform their tasks [25]. In such case, an adaptation may be the triggering of an adequate ambient service tailored for to needs of a user, or having an application running in a user's device starting an action, such as a notification for the user. For example, in our scenario, when a presentation starts a user that is inside a conference room could have his smart-phone's ring turned off, while another user that is chatting at the lobby could be notified about the presentation by the ConfComp application, executing on his notebook.

There are several definitions for context and context-awareness, but one of the most referenced ones can be found in [23]: *"Any information which can be used to characterize the situation of an entity. An entity is a person, a place or an object which is considered relevant for the interaction between a user and an application, including the user and the application."* In an attempt to classify context, Chen and Kotz [19] identified four basic types of context: computational context (i.e., state of resources at the device and of the network), user context (i.e., persons, places and objects), physical context (e.g., luminosity, noise, temperature) and temporal context (e.g., time of the day, period of the year, etc.). Abowd et al. [2] proposed the notions of *primary context* (localization, identity, activity and time) and of *secondary context*, where the latter one can be deduced from the former one and may be used for making adaptation decisions at a higher level of abstraction.

Conceptually, context provisioning can be organized in three layers [43]: *data acquisition and distribution*, *interpretation* and *utilization*. The *data acquisition and distribution layer* is responsible for acquiring raw context data from sensors and devices, which need to be interpreted and evaluated with respect to its accuracy, stability and reliability before it can be utilized. The *interpretation layer* is responsible for this operation, and may combine context data from different sources to enhance its reliability or completeness. For that reason, this layer is in charge of performing context reasoning—the focus of this work—as will be discussed in Sect. 2.5. The *utilization layer* helps applications to select appropriate actions and adaptations based on the available context information and supports the interactions of the applications with other components of the context-aware system. To reduce the complexity of developing context-aware applications, such systems adopt middleware infrastructures for addressing context provisioning tasks [36].

For applications to be able to select, describe and manage context-aware adaptations—or trigger services and actions—the applications and the middleware infrastructure have to share a context model. A context model consists in a formal representation used to describe the context information in context-aware systems, so that every piece of context data may be defined, stored and exchanged in a machine processable form [10]. Strang and Linnhoff-Popien [61] identified and compared six types of context models: attribute-value pairs, schema-based models, graphic models, logic-based models, object-oriented models and ontology-based models. The author's main conclusion is that the object-oriented and the ontology-based models are the most complete and expressive ones, and hence are the most suited for modeling context for ubiquitous computing.

Our Assumption

In our scenario, the context information is represented by data available both at the user's devices, such as his location and preferences, and at the ambient infrastructure, such as the list of activities and its status (e.g., a session that is about to start), the room assigned for each activity and the personnel involved. As a means of describing context information involving aspects of the physical environment, computational resources and social aspects, we adopted an ontology-based model, as will be discussed in the next section.

2.4 Ontology-Based Context Model

An ontology is a formal, explicit description of the concepts in a particular domain of discourse. It provides a vocabulary for representing domain knowledge and for describing specific situations in a domain. An ontology-based approach for context modeling lets us describe context information semantically and share a common understanding of this information among users, devices and services. The main benefits of this sort of model are (a) enabling the reuse of models, (b) enabling the sharing of common knowledge among several applications [59], and (c) allowing the use of formal analysis of the domain knowledge, such as performing context reasoning to deduce high-level contextual information [68].

Ontologies are semantically rich languages, i.e., have great expression power and means of abstraction. As such, they can express all the relationships, models and diagrams defined by taxonomies [54], relational database schemas [70] or a OO software models [34], as well as n-ary relations, constraints, rules and other differentiators including negation and disjunction [28]. Therefore ontologies have been preferred over other conceptual modeling approaches for representing context information in ubiquitous systems [44].

To ensure effective information sharing among devices, ontologies need to be formal and expressive enough to establish a common terminology that guarantees consistent interpretation [15]. The formalism of choice in ontology-based models of context is typically OWL–DL [40], which is becoming a de facto standard in various application domains and is supported by a number of reasoning services [4]. OWL–DL ontologies map directly to Description Logics (DL) [8], a successful family of logic-based knowledge representation formalisms—consisting in decidable fragments of First Order Logic (FOL)—which can be used to represent the conceptual knowledge of an application domain in a structured and formally well-understood way. As such, it has been employed in various application domains, such as natural language processing, configuration, databases or bio-medical ontologies [9], and also in smart spaces ontologies [21].

Differently from FOL, DL explicitly distinguishes between the terminological knowledge (or schema) and the concrete situation [16]. As such, a DL knowledge base—or ontology—consists of two parts: a *terminological part*, the *TBox*, which defines concepts and states additional constraints on the interpretation of these concepts, and an *assertional part*, the *ABox*, which describes individuals and their relationship to each other and to concepts [9]. A TBox comprises (a) *classes*, which represent the concepts of the domain, (b) *properties* that characterize these concepts (*datatype properties*) or define valid relationships between concepts (*object properties*); and (c) *axioms*, which are restrictions applicable to certain elements of the ontology and necessary for a complete description of the knowledge domain. An ABox consists of (a) *individuals* (or instances), defining the concrete elements of a domain associated with every concept in a TBox; and (b) *facts*, or assertions, which associate individuals with specific classes (*unary predicates*) or establish correlations between individuals (*binary predicates*) based on the properties defined in the TBox [38]. In a context-aware system, these facts are used to represent the context data.

For example, in an ontology about the domain of Mobile Devices, the TBox could possibly contain the class *Smart-phone*, which could have as a object property *hasCompany*, indicating the *Company* that builds it, being this another class of the ontology. A possible restriction could state that a *Smart-phone* must have always exactly one *Company* related to it by the property *hasCompany*. As to the ABox, it could contain *SP-1* as an individual of the *Smart-phone* class, defining a specific device in a domain of application, *Nokia* could be an individual of the *Company* class, while *hasCompany(SP-1, Nokia)* would be a fact—a binary predicate in this case—correlating these two individuals, asserting that *SP-1* was manufactured by *Nokia*.

The use of OWL–DL greatly facilitates the modeling of a particular domain of knowledge. Ontologies may be fully described by defining classes, properties, individuals, characteristics of individuals (datatype properties), and relations between individuals (object properties), written manually or with the help of ontology editors, such as Protégé [51]. Complex descriptions of classes and properties can be built by composing elementary descriptions through specific operators provided by OWL–DL [11]. Besides that, an ontology not always has to be entirely described from scratch, as ontologies may be reused or extended to model similar domains. Moreover, OWL–DL ontologies can be verified/classified with the aid of inference mechanisms, e.g., RACER [32] and FaCT [63], for consistency checks, classification and discovery/inference of new information.

In highly dynamic and heterogeneous environments, such as AmI, where different entities may join and leave the environment unforeseeingly, the use of ontologies brings two additional benefits. First, applying ontology integration techniques [18], an ontology that represents a given domain can be dynamically composed from the ontologies that describe the domains of the different interacting elements. In our scenario, for instance, the context of a professor, represented in a *university ontology*, who is inside a room, represented in a *conference center ontology*, carrying a smartphone, represented in a *device ontology*, could be represented by the composition of these three ontologies. Second, as different entities are very likely to employ different knowledge representations, ontology alignment techniques [14] are needed to allow that such representations may be aligned into a single one that can be shared by applications and services.

Our Assumption

To model our AmI system, we took into account not only the physical space (e.g., the modeling of conference rooms, locations) and the availability of resources (e.g., the device's battery level or the quality of network connectivity), but also the social context [64], describing organizational aspects (e.g., sections or departments of a company), users' roles (e.g., professor, student), personal preferences (e.g., the preferred light intensity in a presentation room) and activities (e.g., a presentation, a meeting). Our generic ontology extends the one proposed by Felicíssimo in [27] and comprises six basic classes (or concepts) that represent separate contextual scopes: *Person, Device, Environment, Organization, Role* and *Activity*.

Class *Environment* describes generic physical spaces, e.g., places such as buildings or rooms. As such, subclasses of *Environment* may describe specific kinds of spaces that are common to different organizations, such as a *Classroom* or *Office*, for

Fig. 2.1 The context generic
ontology

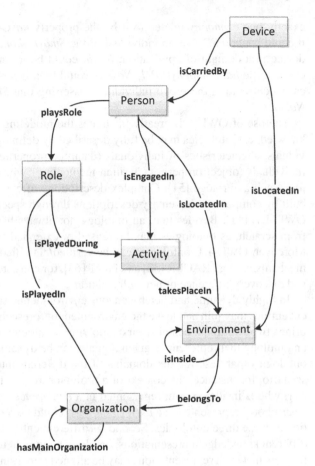

example. Class *Device* describes the characteristics of the computational devices. Its mandatory subclasses are *Mobile Device*, which may comprise subclasses such as *PDA*, *Smartphone*, *Netbook*, etc., and *Fixed Device*, that describes a stationary host. The class *Organization* describes some social structure or institution, like a university or a company, that may have as subclass a department, or an admission office, for example. Class *Role* describes some social or professional function attached to a given individual while class *Person* describes the personal characteristics and preferences of an individual. Finally, class *Activity* describes individual or group tasks in which a person may be engaged.

Figure 2.1 shows a diagram that represents the main classes and properties of the generic ontology. While the classes represent the types of concrete elements that may be enumerated in the system, the properties qualify these elements and are intrinsically related to the context infrastructure. For example, the property *isLocatedIn* is associated with context providers that are capable of determining the position of each device, while the property *isEngagedIn* expresses a situation in which a person may be involved.

This generic ontology works as a general schema. In each case, in order to describe a particular domain or scenario, initially the generic ontology may be extended with new classes, subclasses and properties that are appropriate for the respective scenario. Then it must be instantiated with the definition of specific individuals of that domain. In our scenario, for example, first we defined the new class *Subject*, that is specific for the domain of a conference event. When describing specific elements, *Conference_Center*, *Room_A* and *Room_B* are instances of the class *Environment*. We can model *University* and *Department* as subclasses of *Organization*, and depict *PUC-Rio* as an instance of subclass *University*, and *Informatics* as an instance of subclass *Department*. The classes *Conference* and *Session* would be a subclasses of *Activity*, *UbiConference* an instance of *Conference*, and *Middleware_Session* an instance of *Session*. *Chair* would be a subclass of Role and *Middleware_Session_Chair* an instance of *Chair*, and so on.

Figure 2.2a shows the entities and their relations corresponding to a subset of the scenario described in Sect. 2.1 and according to the adopted ontology adopted in this work. It shows Professor *Silva* (*Person* instance), a *Lecturer* (Role instance) in the *Informatics* department of *PUC-Rio* (*Organization* instances) and also a *Programme_Committee_Member* (*Role* instance) at the *UbiConference* (*Activity* instance). In the *Middleware_Session* (*Activity* instance), which is taking place in *Room_A* (*Environment* instance), *Silva* is the *Chair* (*Role* instance). He carries with him his *Smartphone* and his *Notebook* (*Device* instances). In Fig. 2.2b we see the detailed description of the *Panel_Session_1*, which has *Privacy* as *Subject*, but where the target audience comprises also researchers that are interested in *Security* issues.

2.5 Context Reasoning

In AmI systems, as in any ubiquitous system, reasoning is required for several purposes. First, it is useful to deal with the intrinsic imperfection and uncertainty of context data. Henricksen and Indulska [35] have characterized four kinds of context imperfectness: unknown, ambiguous, imprecise and erroneous. In this case, the main tasks of reasoning are to detect possible errors, make estimates about missing values, determine the quality and validity of the context data. Second, reasoning may also be used for determining higher-level context information, i.e., to infer new, implicit context information, derived from other context data, which may be meaningful and relevant for many applications [24]. Context can be divided into lower-level (primary or raw) context and higher-level (or secondary) context. In general, lower-level context is simple and corresponds to raw data directly collected from sensors or other sources. On the other hand, higher-level context is abstract and needs to be inferred from a set of low-level context [29]. Third, reasoning is fundamental for identifying specific situations, where a situations are regarded as particular combinations of aggregated context data [6], which are relevant for triggering actions or adapta-

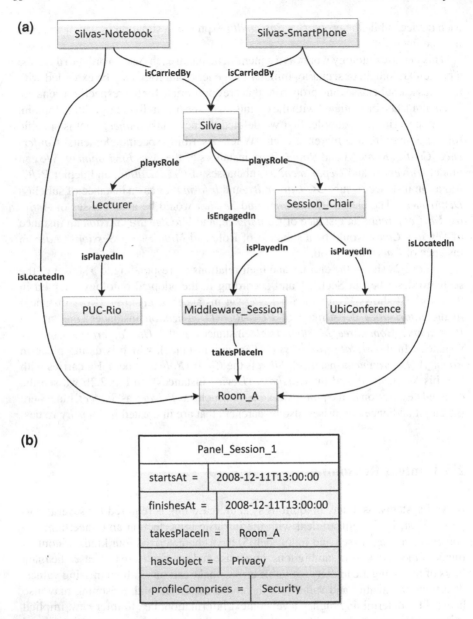

Fig. 2.2 Ontology instances representing the proposed scenario, represented using the Protégé editor

tions in applications or services [71]. A situation itself can bee seen as a specific piece of higher-level context information that serves as an abstraction for application developers [23].

According to Nurmi and Floréen [52], reasoning for context-aware systems can be approached from four main perspectives: the *low-level perspective*, which includes basic tasks such as data pre-processing, data fusion and context inference, usually performed by the sensors or the middleware, the *application-oriented perspective*, where the application can use a wide variety of reasoning methods to process the context data, the *context monitoring perspective*, where the main concern is a correct and efficient update of the knowledge base as the context changes and, finally, the *model monitoring perspective*, where the main task is to continuously evaluate and update learned context classifiers/interpreters and their models, also taking into account user feedback. Although this classification gives an interesting perspective on context reasoning, in AmI environments, we understand that, instead of four perspectives, these are in fact complementary tasks that should be present in every approach for reasoning in such context-aware systems, where context data changes dynamically and inference has to be continuously performed to trigger actions and adaptations.

The reasoning solutions are intrinsically dependent on the context model used by a system. In [12], Bikakis et al. grouped into three approaches the context reasoning solutions adopted by systems that use the ontology-based model: *ontological reasoning*, *rule-based reasoning* and *distributed reasoning*. *Ontological reasoning* is supported by ontology languages like OWL–DL, that can be mapped to certain classes of description logics. In this case, reasoning services are based on subsumption computation for these logics and usually include consistency and classification, as well as checking for instances of specific concepts based on their properties [3]. It may also infer knowledge from ontology axioms. In this case, a reasoner may be used to validate consistency within one ontology and "complete" the ontologies by computing implicit hierarchies and relationships based on given axioms [62].

In the *rule-based reasoning*, derivation rules are used to describe higher-level context information or specific situations based on several pieces of context information. These rules may be written in different types of logic, such as first order logic, temporal logic, description logic or fuzzy logic [42], for instance, and may be defined by the application developers or system's users, or identified using specialized techniques, such as machine learning techniques.

Distributed reasoning employs methods and techniques from the field of Distributed Artificial Intelligence to cope with the elements that collect, store, process, exchange and reason about context data in distributed, context-aware, systems [12]. These three approaches are not mutually exclusive. In fact, rule-based reasoning complements ontology-based reasoning, while both approaches are complemented by distributed reasoning techniques to deal with the physical distribution of computing and sensor devices, context providers and consumers, entities responsible for brokering and reasoning, and/or applications and users that may potentially engage into spontaneous collaboration.

Our Assumption

In this work, we focus only on rule-based and distributed reasoning approaches. In our scenario, the ConfOrg service, executing on the ambient infrastructure, and the ConfComp application, running on the notebook of professor Silva, rely on a two-tier context reasoning service capable of cooperatively identifying the situations (or contexts) that are of interest to the AmI application. For example, when a session is about to start and Silva is reading e-mails at the lobby, the ConfComp could open a pop up window to alert Silva that a session is going to start, and that he might want to go to the respective room. This situation may be described by an inference rule (rule-based reasoning). The overall context information that characterizes this situation is distributed among the ambient infrastructure (session schedule) and Silva's device (his preference and his location).

2.6 Rule-Based Reasoning

Derivation rules are essentially a mean for calculating a derived value of data on-the-fly, often by employing some simple kind of table lookup in a database. They are a technology often used to provide views of stored data in databases [49], i.e., describing a data query. As discussed in the previous section, rule-based reasoning consists in the use of derivation rules, based on some type of logic, to describe and infer higher-level context data or specific situations. Dey [23] presents the *situation abstraction* as a powerful feature in the design of context-aware systems: "*providing the description of the states of relevant entities in a system in the form of a* situation abstraction *requires less effort than determining which individual context components need to be contacted and determining when the collective situation has been realized or satisfied, allowing context-aware application designers to concentrate on the heart of the design process.*" As such, providing rule-based inference mechanisms may be regarded as an important requirement for middleware to support the development and deployment of AmI systems.

The use of rules to describe specific situations has also some great advantages. First, rules languages (e.g., SWRL [41], CARIN [46], RDQL [58]) provide a formal model for describing situations and performing context reasoning. As such, rule-based formalisms consist in a popular paradigm of knowledge representation [45]. The expressivity and complexity of rule languages have been studied extensively, and many decidable and tractable formalisms are known. Second, while other reasoning approaches (e.g., Bayesian or neural networks) have to be designed specifically to perform one type of inference, the use of rules brings great flexibility, as rules may be reused or easily modified by application developers to represent similar situations. Besides that, rules may be previously loaded on the start up of applications or middleware services, or even defined by means of intelligent users interfaces or learning techniques and provided dynamically. Third, rules are easy to understand and widespread used, and there are many systems that integrate them with the ontology-based model [12]. With the increasingly adoption of ontology-based context model, the use of ontological reasoning together with rule-based reasoning has gained in interest, for the addition of rules to ontological knowledge confers additional expressiveness on the context model [37]. That happens because, for reasons of decidability, DL ontological reasoning currently not allows the composition of properties. As in many applications this is a useful operation, such integration of rule-based knowledge representation and DL ontologies is currently an active area of research [40].

Our Assumption

Our DL-safe rules are based on the SWRL rule language [53]. They take the form of a conjunctive query, which consists in an implication between an antecedent (body) and a consequent (head). The intended meaning can be read as: whenever the conditions specified in the antecedent holds, then the conditions specified in the consequent must also hold. Both the antecedent and the consequent are composed of atoms, each of which represents valid unary or binary predicates in the TBox, i.e., atoms in these rules can be of the form $C(x)$, $P(x, y)$, where C is an class name, P is property name, and x and y are either variables or valid individual names in the ABox.

In this work, we focus on checking individuals, a fundamental reasoning task with respect to an ABox. In other words, we are concerned with the inference of class assertions and property assertions [30] to determine a set of individuals that satisfy the rule. The consequent lists variables for which the user would like to compute bindings, while the antecedent consists of atoms in which all variables from the consequent must be mentioned, but that may contain additional variables, assumed as existentially quantified. The result of the reasoning operation for such rule, i.e., the query answer, is a set of tuples representing bindings for variables mentioned in the consequent [31]. Essentially, the possible values that free variables may assume are restricted to named individuals only, confining the evaluation of such rules to the ABox. This safety condition is known as "DL-safety" and such rules are generally called "DL-safe rules." Not only are DL-safe rules decidable, but they can be solved by the available reasoner implementations [39].

Rule 2.1:

$$takesPlaceIn(?x, ?y) \land hasStarted(?x) \Rightarrow isBusy(?y)$$

Using the standard textual notation for DL rules, of the form *antecedent* ⇒ *consequent*, an example of a rule asserting that "when session X that takes place in room Y has already started it implies that room Y is busy" would be written as in Rule 2.1, in which the variables are indicated in the standard convention of using a question mark prefix (e.g., ?x). If, for example, the ABox contained the facts *takesPlaceIn(Middleware_Session, Room_A)*, *takesPlaceIn(AmI_Session, Room_B)*, *takesPlaceIn(Privacy_Session, Room_C)*, *hasStarted(Middleware_Session)* and *hasStarted(Privacy_Session)*, the result for the rule would be the set {*Room_A*, *Room_C*}, indicating that the predicate *isBusy* is valid for both individuals.

2.7 Discussion

In this chapter, initially we described our motivating scenario, a fictitious conference that takes place in a facility enriched with AmI technology. While the attendees and organizers of the conference move through different spaces carrying one or more mobile devices, applications executing on their devices autonomously interact with different ambient services. These applications and services are context-aware and their actions are triggered based on context information collected both from the user's devices, such as his location and preferences, and the ambient infrastructure, such as the room assigned for each activity and its status. For describing this context information, we adopted an ontology-based model, in order to be able to represent not only aspects of the physical environment and computational resources but also the social aspects, such as personal preferences and activities of the users.

Applications in our scenario, such as the ConfOrg service, running on the ambient infrastructure, and the ConfComp application, running on the notebook of professor Silva, rely on a context reasoning service capable of identifying the situations in which specific actions have to be triggered. For example, when a session is about to start and Silva is reading e-mails at the lobby, the ConfComp should open a pop up window to warn Silva to go to the respective room. These situations are described using derivation rules. The context information that characterizes this situation, though, is distributed between the ambient infrastructure and Silva's device, which makes necessary the use of some distributed reasoning approach.

In the next chapter, we discuss and compare some frameworks and middleware systems that deal with distributed reasoning.

References

1. Aarts, E., de Ruyter, B.: New research perspectives on Ambient Intelligence. J. Ambient Intell. Smart Environ. **1**(1), 5–14 (2009). doi:10.3233/AIS-2009-0001
2. Abowd, G., Dey, A., Brown, P., Davies, N., Smith, M., Steggles, P.: Towards a better understanding of context and context-awareness. In: Proceeding of the 1st International Symposium on Handheld and Ubiquitous Computing (HUC 99), pp. 304–307. Springer, London (1999)
3. Agostini, A., Bettini, C., Riboni, D.: Loosely coupling ontological reasoning with an efficient middleware for context-awareness. In: Proceedings of the The Second Annual International Conference on Mobile and Ubiquitous Systems: Networking and Services (MOBIQUITOUS '05), pp. 175–182. IEEE Computer Society, Washington, DC (2005). doi:10.1109/MOBIQUITOUS.2005.34
4. Agostini, A., Bettini, C., Riboni, D.: A performance evaluation of ontology-based context reasoning. In: Proceedings of the Fifth IEEE International Conference on Pervasive Computing and Communications Workshops (PERCOMW '07), pp. 3–8. IEEE Computer Society, Washington, DC (2007). doi:10.1109/PERCOMW.2007.10
5. Ahola, J.: Ambient Intelligence. Final report, Ist Advisory Group (2001)
6. Anagnostopoulos, C.B., Hadjiefthymiades, S.: Enhancing situation-aware systems through imprecise reasoning. IEEE Trans. Mobile Comput. **7**(10), 1153–1168 (2008)

7. Augusto, J., McCullagh, P., Croft, V., Walkden, J.A.: Enhanced healthcare provision through assisted decision-making in a smart home environment. In: Proceedings of 2nd Workshop on Artificial Intelligence Techniques for Ambient Intelligence (AITAmI07), pp. 27–32 (2007)
8. Baader, F., Calvanese, D., McGuinness, D., Nardi, D., Patel-Schneider, P.: The Description Logic Handbook. Cambridge University Press, London (2003)
9. Baader, F., Sertkaya, B.: Usability issues in description logic knowledge base completion. In: S. Ferré, S. Rudolph (eds.) Proceedings of the 7th International Conference on Formal Concept Analysis, (ICFCA 2009), Lecture Notes in Artificial Ingelligence, vol. 5548, pp. 1–21. Springer, Heidelberg (2009)
10. Baldauf, M., Dustdar, S., Rosenberg, F.: A survey on context-aware systems. Int. J. Ad Hoc Ubiquitous Comput. 2(4), 263–277 (2007)
11. Bettini, C., Brdiczka, O., Henricksen, K., Indulska, J., Nicklas, D., Ranganathan, A., Riboni, D.: A survey of context modelling and reasoning techniques. Pervasive and Mobile Computing In Press, Corrected Proof-(2009). doi:10.1016/j.pmcj.2009.06.002. http://www.sciencedirect.com/science/article/B7MF1-4WGMBDB-1/2/1230418cb6af35d6b58e0514adff2680
12. Bikakis, A., Patkos, T., Antoniou, G., Plexousakis, D.: A survey of semantics-based approaches for context reasoning in ambient intelligence. In: Bergmann, R., Althoff, K.D., Furbach, U., Schmid, K. (eds.) Proceedings of the Workshop "Artificial Intelligence Methods for Ambient Intelligence" at the European Conference on Ambient Intelligence (AmI'07), pp. 15–24 (2007)
13. Bohn, J., Coroama, V., Langheinrich, M., Mattern, F., Rohs, M.: Social, economic, and ethical implications of ambient intelligence and ubiquitous computing. In: Weber, W., Rabaey, J., Aarts, E. (eds.) Ambient Intelligence, pp. 5–29. Springer, Berlin (2005)
14. Breitman, K., Felicíssimo, C., Casanova, M.: CATO—A lightweight ontology alignment tool. In: Belo, O., Eder, J., e Cunha, J.F., Pastor, O. (eds.) CAiSE Short Paper Proceedings, CEUR Workshop Proceedings, vol. 161. (2005). http://CEUR-WS.org
15. Breitman, K., M.Hinchey: The use of formal ontology to specify context in ubiquitous computing. In: Margaria, T., Steffen, B. (eds.) Proceedings of the 3rd International Symposium on Leveraging Applications of Formal Methods, Verification and Validation (ISoLA 2008), vol. 17, pp. 561–571 (2008)
16. Bunningen, A.H.: Context aware querying—Challenges for data management in ambient intelligence.Technical Report, Department of EEMCS, University of Twente, The Netherlands, (2004)
17. Cabitza, F., Locatelli, M., Sarini, M., Simone, C.: CASMAS: Supporting collaboration in pervasive environments. In: Proceedings of the 4th Annual IEEE International Conference on Pervasive Computing and Communications (PerCom 2006), pp. 286–295 (2006)
18. Cafezeiro, I., Viterbo, J., Rademaker, A., Haeusler, E., Endler, M.: A formal framework for modeling context—aware behavior in ubiquitous computing. In: Proceedings of the 3rd International Symposium on Leveraging Applications of Formal Methods, Verification and Validation (ISoLA 2008), pp. 519–533 (2008)
19. Chen, G., Kotz, D.: A survey of context-aware mobile computing research. Technical Report. TR2000-381, Department of Computer Science, Dartmouth College (2000)
20. Chen, H., Finin, T., Joshi, A.: A context broker for building smart meeting rooms. In: Proceedings of the Knowledge Representation and Ontology for Autonomous Systems Symposium, pp. 53–60 (2004)
21. Chen, H., Perich, F., Finin, T., Joshi, A.: SOUPA: Standard ontology for ubiquitous and pervasive applications. In: Proceedings of the 1st Annual International Conference on Mobile and Ubiquitous Systems (MobiQuitous 2004), pp. 258–267 (2004)
22. Cook, D., Augusto, J., Jakkula, V.: Ambient intelligence: Technologies, applications, and opportunities. Pervasive Mobile Comput. 5, 277–298 (2009)
23. Dey, A.: Understanding and Using Context. Pers. Ubiquitous Comput. 5(1), 4–7 (2001)
24. Dey, A., Salber, D., Abowd, G.: A conceptual framework and a toolkit for supporting the rapid prototyping of context-aware applications. Hum. Comput. Interact. 16(1), 97–166 (2001)
25. Ducatel, K., Bogdanowicz, M., Scapolo, F., Leijten, J., Burgelma, J.C.: Scenarios for ambient intelligence in 2010. Final report, IST Advisory Group (2001)

26. Emiliani, P., Stephanidis, C.: Universal access to ambient intelligence environments: opportunities and challenges for people with disabilities. IBM Syst. J. **44**(3), 605–619 (2005)
27. Felicíssimo, C., Chopinaud, C., Briot, J.P., Seghrouchni, A., Lucena, C.: Contextualizing normative open multi-agent systems. In: Proceedings of 23rd Annual ACM Symposium on Applied Computing (SAC 2008), vol. 1, pp. 52–59 (2008)
28. Gómez-Pérez, A., Fernadéz-Peréz, M., Corcho, O.: Ontological Engineering. Springer, London (2004)
29. Guan, D., Yuan, W., Cho, S., Gavrilov, A., Lee, Y.K., Lee, S.: Devising a context selection-based reasoning engine for context-aware ubiquitous computing middleware. In:Indulska, J., Ma, J., Yang, L.T., Ungerer, T., Cao, J. (eds.) UIC, Lecture Notes in Computer Science, vol. 4611, pp. 849–857. Springer, Heidelberg (2007). http://dblp.uni-trier.de/db/conf/uic/uic2007.html#GuanYCGLL07
30. Guo, Y., Heflin, J.: A scalable approach for partitioning OWL knowledge bases. In: Proceedings of the 2nd International Workshop on Scalable Semantic Web Knowledge Base Systems (SSWS 2006), pp. 47–60 (2006)
31. Haarslev, V.: Möller, R.: On the scalability of description logic instance retrieval. J. Autom. Reason. **41**(2), 99–142 (2008). doi:10.1007/s10817-008-9104-7
32. Haarslev, V., Möller, R.: RACER system description. In: Proceedings of the International Joint Conference on Automated Reasoning (IJCAR'01), Lecture Notes in Computer Science, vol. 2083 (2001)
33. Hefley, W., Murray, D.: Intelligent user interfaces. In: Proceedings of the 1st International Conference on Intelligent User Interfaces (IUI'93), pp. 3–10. ACM, New York (1993). doi:10.1145/169891.169892
34. Henderson-Sellers, B., Barbier, F.: What is this thing called aggregation? In: Proceedings of the Technology of Object-Oriented Languages and Systems (TOOLS'99), p. 236. IEEE Computer Society, Washington, DC (1999)
35. Henricksen, K., Indulska, J.: Modelling and using imperfect context information. In: Proceedings of the Second IEEE Annual Conference on Pervasive Computing and Communications Workshops, IEEE Computer Society, Washington, DC (2004)
36. Henricksen, K., Indulska, J.: Developing context-aware pervasive computing applications: models and approach. Pervasive Mobile Comput. **2**(1), 37–64 (2006)
37. Heymans, S., Nieuwenborgh, D., Vermeir, D.: Nonmonotonic ontological and rule-based reasoning with extended conceptual logic programs. In: Proceedings of the 2nd European Semantic Web Conference (ESWC 2005), pp. 392–407. Springer, Berlin (2005). doi:10.1007/11431053_27
38. Hilera, J., Ruiz, F.: Ontologies in ubiquitous computing. In: Proceedings of the I International Conference on Ubiquitous Computing: Applications, Technology and Social Issues (ICUC 2006), Madrid, (2006)
39. Hitzler, P., Parsia, B.: Ontologies and Rules. In: Staab, S., Studer, R. (eds.) Handbook on Ontologies, 2nd Edn., Chap. 3, pp. 111–132. Springer, Heidelberg (2009)
40. Horrocks, I., Patel-Schneider, P., Harmelen, F.: From SHIQ and RDF to OWL: The making of a web ontology language. J. Web Semant. **1**(1), 7–26 (2003)
41. Horrocks, I., Patel-Schneider, P.F., Boley, H., Tabet, S., Grosof, B., Dean., M.: SWRL: A semantic web rule language combining owl and ruleml. W3C member submission (2004)
42. Jie, S., ZhaoHui, W.: Context reasoning technologies in ubiquitous computing environment. In: Proceedings of Embedded and Ubiquitous Computing (EUC 2006), Seoul, pp. 1027–1036 (2006)
43. Jones, G.: Challenges and opportunities of context-aware information access. In: UDM '05: Proceedings of the International Workshop on Ubiquitous Data Management, pp. 53–62. IEEE Computer Society, Washington, DC (2005). doi:10.1109/UDM.2005.5
44. Breitman, K., Casanova, M.A., Truszkowski, W.: Semantic Web: Concepts, Technologies and Applications. Springer, New York (2007)
45. Krötzsch, M., Rudolph, S., Hitzler, P.: Description logic rules. In: Proceedings of the 18th European Conference on Artificial Intelligence (ECAI2008), Patras, July 2008. pp. 80–84. IOS Press, Amsterdam (2008)

46. Levy, A., Rousset, M.C.: Combining horn rules and description logics in CARIN. Artifi. Intell. 104(1–2), 165–209 (1998). doi:10.1016/S0004-3702(98)00048-4
47. Lindenberg, J., Pasman, W., Kranenborg, K.: J. Stegeman, Neerincx, M.: Improving service matching and selection in ubiquitous computing environments: a user study. Pers. Ubiquitous Comput. 11(1), 59–68 (2006)
48. Maña, A., Rudolph, C., Spanoudakis, G., Lotz, V., Massacci, F., López-Cobo, M.M.J.M.: Security engineering for ambient intelligence: a manifesto. In: Integrating Security and Software Engineering: Advances and Future Vision, pp. 244–270. Idea Group Publishing, Hershey (2006)
49. McKenzie, C., Gray, P., Preece, A.: Extending SWRL to express fully-quantified constraints. In: Proceedings of the 3rd International Workshop on Rules and Rule Markup Languages for the Semantic Web (RuleML 2004), pp. 139–154. Springer, Berlin (2004). doi:10.1007/b102922
50. Nehmer, J., Becker, M., Karshmer, A., Lamm, R.: Living assistance systems: an ambient intelligence approach. In: Proceedings of the 28th international conference on Software engineering (ICSE '06), Shanghai, May 2006. pp. 43–50 (2006)
51. Noy, N., Sintek, M., Decker, S., Crubézy, M., Fergerson, R., Musen, M.: Creating semantic web contents with protégé-2000. IEEE Intell. Syst. 16(2), 60–71 (2001). doi:10.1109/5254.920601
52. Nurmi, P., Floreen, P.: Reasoning in context-aware Systems. http://www.cs.helsinki.fi/u/ptnurmi/papers/positionpaper.pdf (2004)
53. O'Connor, M., Knublauch, H., Tu, S., Grosof, B., Dean, M., Grosso, W., Musen, M.: Supporting rule system interoperability on the semantic web with SWRL. The Semantic Web-ISWC 2005. Lecture Notes in Computer Science, vol. 3729, pp. 974–986. Springer, Heidelberg (2005)
54. Peckham, J., Maryanski, F.: Semantic data models. ACM Comput. Surv. 20(3), 153–189 (1988). doi:10.1145/62061.62062
55. Raisinghani, M., Benoit, A., Ding, J., Gomez, M., Gupta, K., Gusila, V., Power, D., Schmedding, O.: Ambient intelligence: changing forms of human-computer interaction and their social implications. J. Digit. Inf. 5(4), Article no. 271 (2004)
56. Riva, G.: Ambient intelligence in health care. CyberPsychol. Behavior 6(3), 295–300 (2003)
57. Román, M., Hess, C., Cerqueira, R., Ranganathan, A., Campbell, R., Nahrstedt, K.: A middleware infrastructure for active spaces. IEEE Pervasive Comput. 1(4), 74–83 (2002)
58. Seaborne, A.: A query language for RDF. W3C member submission (2004)
59. Shehzad, A., Ngo, H., Pham, K., Lee, S.: Formal modeling in context aware systems. In: Proceedings of the First International Workshop on Modeling and Retrieval of Context, (2004)
60. Soldatos, J., Dimakis, N., Stamatis, K., Polymenakos, L.: A breadboard architecture for pervasive context-aware services in smart spaces: middleware components and prototype applications. Pers. Ubiquitous Comput. J. 11(3), 193–212 (2007). doi:10.1007/s00779-006-0102-7
61. Strang, T., Linnhoff-Popien, C.: A context modeling survey. In: First International Workshop on Advanced Context Modelling, Reasoning and Management. Nottingham, (2004)
62. Strang, T., Linnhoff-Popien, C., Frank, K.: CoOL: a context ontology language to enable contextual interoperability distributed applications and interoperable systems. LNCS 2893, 236–247 (2003)
63. Tsarkov, D., Horrocks, I.: FaCT++ description logic reasoner: system description. In: Proceedings of the International Joint Conference on Automated Reasoning (IJCAR 2006), Lecture Notes in Artificial Intelligence, vol. 4130, pp. 292–297. Springer, Heidelberg (2006). http://download/2006/TsHo06a.pdf
64. Viterbo, J., Felicíssimo, C., Briot, J.P., Endler, M., Lucena, C.: Applying regulation to ubiquitous computing environments. In: Proceedings of the 2nd Workshop on Software Engineering for Agent-oriented Systems (SEAS 06), pp. 107–118 (2006)
65. Viterbo, J., Mazuel, L., Charif, Y., Endler, M., Sabouret, N., Breitman, K., Seghrouchni, A., Briot, J.P.: Ambient intelligence: management of distributed and heterogeneous context knowledge. In: W. Dargie (ed.) Context-Aware Computing and Self-Managing Systems, Chap. 4, pp. 79–128. CRC/Francis and Taylor, New York, (2009)

66. Viterbo, J., Sacramento, V., Rocha, R., Baptista, G., Malcher, M., Endler, M.: A middleware architecture for context-aware and location-based mobile applications. In: Proceedings of 32nd Annual IEEE Software Engineering Workshop (SEW-32). IEEE Computer Society (2008)

67. Wang, X., Dong, J., Chin, C., Hettiarachchi, S., Zhang, D.: Semantic space: an infrastructure for smart spaces. Pervasive Comput. **3**(3), 32–39 (2004)

68. Wang, X., Zhang, D., Gu, T., Pung, H.: Ontology based context modeling and reasoning using OWL. In: Proceedings of 2nd IEEE Conference on Pervasive Computing and Communications (PerCom 2004), Workshop on Context Modeling and Reasoning, pp. 18–22. IEEE Computer Society Press, Orlando, (2004)

69. Weiser, M.: Some computer science issues in ubiquitous computing. ACM SIGMOBILE Mobile Comput. Commun. Rev. **3**(3), 12 (1999). doi:10.1145/329124.329127

70. Xu, Z., Zhang, S., Dong, Y.: Mapping between relational database schema and OWL ontology for deep annotation. In: Proceedings of the 2006 IEEE/WIC/ACM International Conference on Web Intelligence (WI'06), pp. 548–552. IEEE Computer Society, Washington, DC (2006). doi:10.1109/WI.2006.114

71. Yau, S.S., Huang, D., Gong, H., Seth, S.: Development and runtime support for situation-aware application software in ubiquitous computing environments. In: Proceedings of the 28th Annual International Computer Software and Applications Conference (COMPSAC'04), pp. 452–457 (2004)

Chapter 3
Related Work

Abstract In this chapter, we present several different approaches for distributed reasoning in AmI environments and discuss the advantages and disadvantages of these systems.

Keywords Ambient Intelligence · Ubiquitous computing · Context-awareness · Middleware · Ontology · Distributed reasoning

3.1 Distributed Reasoning

Middleware systems that give support to ubiquitous computing environments traditionally adopt a centralized approach for their reasoning mechanisms [2], in which a central entity is responsible for collecting the available context data from all sensors and ambient software entities operating in the same environment, and for all the required reasoning tasks, which may include transforming the imported context data in a common format, deducing higher-level context information form the raw context data, and taking context-oriented decisions for the behavior of the system [3]. This is the case of CoBrA [7], CHIL [17] and Semantic Space [18], for example.

However, in AmI environments, applications, services, rules and context information may be partially or fully distributed among the different elements involved. Thus in some circumstances a centralized approach may be inefficient and even infeasible—e.g., if not all context information is available at the node in charge of reasoning. In such environments, distributed reasoning is necessary to address the complexity that arises from the coexistence of different elements that collect, store, process, exchange and reason about context data [4]. Hence, there are some approaches for distributed reasoning that try to overcome this limitation, such as Gaia [13], OWL-SF [10], DRAGO [15], P2P-DR [2] and P2PIS [1]. In the following sections we discuss the main features of each of these aforementioned solutions.

J. Viterbo and M. Endler, *Decentralized Reasoning in Ambient Intelligence*, SpringerBriefs in Computer Science, DOI: 10.1007/978-1-4471-4168-6_3,

3.2 Gaia

Gaia framework aims at providing a generic computational environment to integrate physical spaces and their ubiquitous computing devices into a programmable computing and communication system [11, 13]. It provides core services, including events, entity presence (devices, users and services), discovery and naming. By specifying well-defined interfaces to services, applications may be built in a generic way so that they are able to run in arbitrary active spaces.

Gaia's context infrastructure allows applications to obtain a variety of contextual information. Various components, called *Context Providers*, obtain context from either sensors or other data sources. These include sensors that track people's locations, room conditions (for example, temperature and sound) and weather conditions. *Context Providers* allow applications to query them for context information. Some *Context Providers* also have an event channel to asynchronously send context events. Thus, applications can either query a *Context Providers* or listen on the event channel to get context information.

All the ontologies in Gaia are maintained by an *Ontology Server*. Entities contact this server to get descriptions of other entities in the environment, information about context or definitions of various terms used in Gaia. The server also supports semantic queries to get, for example, the classification of individuals or subsumption of concepts. The *Ontology Server* also provides an interface for adding new concepts to existing ontologies.

Reasoning Approach

Context Synthesizers are Gaia components that collect context data from various *Context Providers*, derive higher level or abstract context from these lower-level context data and provide these inferred contexts to applications. Whenever a *Context Synthesizer* deduces a change in the inferred context, it publishes the new information. Gaia adopts two basic inference approaches [12]. *Rule-based Synthesizers* use predefined rules written in first order logic to infer different contexts. Each of the rules also has an associated priority, which is used to choose one rule when multiple rules are valid at the same time. However, if all the valid rules have the same priority, one of them is picked at random. Alternatively, some *Synthesizers* may use machine learning techniques, such as Bayesian learning and reinforcement learning, to infer high-level contexts. Past context information is used to train the learner.

3.3 OWL-SF

The distributed semantic service framework, OWL-SF [10], supports the design of ubiquitous context-aware systems considering both the distributed nature of context information and the heterogeneity of devices that provide services and deliver context. It uses OWL to represent high-level context information in a semantically well-founded form, and its functional architecture integrates two basic building blocks: OWL Super Distributed Objects (OWL-SDOs) and Deduction Servers (DSs). OWL-SDOs are OWL enabled extensions of Super Distributed Objects (SDOs) [14], which encapsulate devices, sensors, user's interfaces (GUIs), services and other environmental entities and connect them to the upper context ontology, communicating using the Representational State Transfer Protocol [8]. Deduction Servers (DSs) are specific OWL-SDOs with an RDF inference mechanism and an OWL-DL reasoner. A system may be composed of multiple components of both types, which can be added and removed dynamically at runtime. DSs use the SDO discovery and announcement implementation to become aware of new SDOs in the environment. Whenever a new SDO is discovered, its semantic representation is added to the internal database.

Each SDO that encapsulates context providers and service-providing devices allows accessing the current state of an object as an OWL description. Each functional entity implemented as OWL-SDO has to be described using its own ontology containing terminological knowledge that enables the automatic classification of the object into appropriate service categories. The state of an object stores context values and is represented by an individual of a class in the ontology. Integrated reasoning facilities perform the automatic verification of the consistency of the provided service specifications and the represented context information, so that the system can detect and rule out faulty service descriptions and can provide reliable situation interpretation.

Reasoning Approach

Deduction servers (DSs) are specific OWL-SDO with an RDF inference mechanism and an OWL-DL reasoner. The rule-based reasoning process is provided by the RDF inference component and the deduced facts are used to trigger events to other SDOs and to process service calls. A subscription notification mechanism is used to monitor the SDO parameters to generate notifications whenever an observed parameter changes, triggering the deduction process to update the global ontology model accordingly. The RDF inference component is connected to the OWL-DL reasoner, which is responsible for classification and answering OWL-DL queries. The Racer system [9] is used as an OWL-DL reasoner. Besides providing deductive support, DSs are responsible for collecting the status of SDOs, published in the OWL format, and building an integrated OWL description accessible to the reasoning process. The semantic representation of each SDO is added to the internal database of the DS. This semantic representation consists of a set of instances augmented with rules. Facts deduced from rules are only used to change parameters and to call services but never modify the knowledge base.

3.4 DRAGO

Distributed Reasoning Architecture for a Galaxy of Ontologies (DRAGO) is a distributed reasoning system implemented as a peer-to-peer architecture, in which every peer registers a set of ontologies and mappings [15]. In DRAGO, the reasoning operations are implemented using local reasoning over each registered ontology and by coordinating with other peers when local ontologies are semantically connected with the ontologies registered in other peers. DRAGO does not implement a context layer, i.e., it does not have any service for context collection, storing or distribution.

DRAGO is implemented to operate over HTTP and access ontologies and mappings published on the web. It aggregates a web of ontologies distributed amongst a peer-to-peer network in which each participant is called a *DRAGO Reasoning Peer* (DRP). A DRP is the basic element of the system and may contain a set of different ontologies describing specific domains of interest (for example, ontologies describing different activities of users in a university). These ontologies may differ from a subjective perspective and level of granularity. In a DRP there are also semantic mappings, each defining semantic relations between entities belonging to two different ontologies, described using C-OWL [5]. As these mappings establish a correlation between the local ontology and ontologies assigned to other DRPs, a DRP may also request reasoning services for other DRPs as part of a distributed reasoning task. Among the reasoning services DRAGO allows to check for ontology consistency, build classifications, verify concepts satisfiability and check entailment.

A DRP has two interfaces that can be invoked by users or applications. A *Registration Service Interface* is available for creating/modifying/deleting registrations of ontologies and mappings assigned to them. A *Reasoning Service Interface* enables requests of reasoning services for registered ontologies. To register an ontology at a peer the user specifies a logical identifier for it, i.e., a URI, and inform a physical location of the ontology in the web. Besides that, it is possible to assign semantic mappings to the ontology, providing, in the same manner, the location of the mappings on the web. New peers may be added dynamically to the system, providing new ontologies and semantic mappings. As each peer registers sets of heterogeneous ontologies and mappings, the knowledge base is totally distributed. When users or applications want to perform reasoning with a registered ontology they refer to the corresponding peer and invoke its reasoning services giving the URI to which the ontology was bound.

Reasoning Approach

The reasoning process in DRAGO may compare concepts in different ontologies to check concept satisfiability, determining if a concept subsumes the other (i.e., the latter is less general than the former), based on the semantic mappings relating both ontologies. In a set of ontologies interconnected with semantic mappings, the inference of concept subsumption in one ontology (or between ontologies) may depend also on other ontologies related to the previous ones through those mappings. Every peer registers a set of ontologies and mappings, and provides reasoning services for ontologies with registered mappings. Each peer may also request reasoning services from other peers when their local ontologies are semantically connected (through a mapping) with the ontologies registered at the other peer. The reasoning with multiple ontologies is performed by a combination of local reasoning operations, internally executed in each peer for each distinct ontology. A distributed tableau algorithm is adopted for checking concept satisfiability in a set of interconnected ontologies by combining local (standard) tableaux procedures that check satisfiability inside the single ontology. Due to the limitations of the distributed tableau algorithm, DRAGO supports only three types of rules connecting atomic concepts in two different ontologies: *is equivalent*, *is subsumed* and *subsumes*. A Distributed Reasoner was implemented as an extension to the open source OWL reasoner Pellet [16].

3.5 P2P-DR

P2P-DR proposes a distributed solution for reasoning about context tailored to the special characteristics of AmI environments. This approach models the entities of an ubiquitous environment as nodes in a P2P system, in which each different node independently collects and processes the available context information. Specifically, it considers nodes that have exclusive knowledge, and that interact with neighbor nodes to exchange context information [2]. The knowledge of each node is expressed in terms of rules, and knowledge is imported from other nodes through bridging rules. As each peer may not have direct access to all sources of information, they share their knowledge through messages with their neighbor nodes. Moreover, the P2P-DR reasoning algorithm models and reasons with potential conflicts that may arise during the integration of the distributed knowledge.

Reasoning Approach

In a P2P-DR system, each peer has some computing and reasoning capabilities that it may use to solve a query about a local literal, based on its local and imported knowledge, which comprises context data and rules. A peer may not be able to solve the query locally, but it is aware of the knowledge that each of the other peers—that it can communicate with—possesses, and has mappings that define how part of this knowledge relates to its local knowledge. As each peer is willing to disclose and share its local knowledge, peers communicate with a subset of the other available peers to import the knowledge necessary to solve the query.

3.6 P2PIS

A peer-to-peer inference system (P2PIS [1]) is a network of peer theories. Each peer has a finite set of propositional formulas and can be semantically related by sharing variables with other peers. A shared variable between two peers is in the intersection of the vocabularies of the two peers. Not all the variables in common in the vocabularies of two peers have to be shared by them. Besides, two peers may not be aware of all the variables that they have in common but only of some of them. In a P2PIS, no peer has the knowledge of the global P2PIS theory. Each peer only knows its own local theory and the variables that it shares with some other peers of the P2PIS (its acquaintances). It does not necessarily knows all the variables that it has in common with other peers (including with its acquaintances). When a new peer joins a P2PIS it simply declares its acquaintances in the P2PIS, i.e., the peers it knows to be sharing variables with, and it declares the corresponding shared variables.

Reasoning Approach

In P2PIS the local theory of each peer is composed of a set of propositional clauses defined upon a set of propositional variables, called its local vocabulary. Each peer may share part of its vocabulary with some other peers. The system is capable of the reasoning task of finding consequences of a certain form (e.g., clauses involving only certain variables) for a given input formula expressed using the local vocabulary of a peer. Other reasoning tasks, e.g., finding implicants of a certain form for a given input formula, can be equivalently reduced to the consequence finding task. P2PIS distributed algorithm splits clauses if they share variables of several peers. Each piece of a split clause is then transmitted to the corresponding theory to find its consequences. The consequences that are found for each piece of split clause must then be re-composed to get the consequences of the clause that had been split.

3.7 Discussion

In this chapter, we discussed the need for distributed reasoning as a direct requirement that arises from the open, dynamic and heterogeneous nature of AmI. We described five proposals for distributed reasoning frameworks that support the deployment of AmI systems and try to overcome the limitation of traditional centralized reasoning approaches: Gaia, OWL-SF, DRAGO, P2P-DR and P2PIS. Among them, it may be said that Gaia and OWL-SF are the ones that best deal with dynamic scenarios, allowing context providers to be added or removed dynamically and ontologies to be dynamically modified with regard to types of context and their properties. Gaia offers a flexible and generic computational environment to fully implement and deploy AmI systems, and OWL-SF may be used for implementing such systems, despite not being tailored specifically for smart spaces, as its singular characteristic is its support for distributed inference. Both frameworks perform rule-based reasoning considering a distributed knowledge base. Moreover, they have two main advantages: (i) they allow event-based communication, so that a rule can be monitored and the result is sent for the subscriber when there is any change; and (ii) they allow the rules to be described with variables, in a more flexible way. In both frameworks, the aggregated context information in each reasoner will depend on the available providers, avoiding communication bottlenecks and allowing more efficient information processing and dissemination. However, the disadvantage of these approaches is that each reasoner is capable of reasoning only about the local context data, i.e., reasoners do not interact to exchange context information. As such, a context consumer has to know beforehand which context information will be available at each reasoner.

In contrast, DRAGO, P2P-DR and P2PIS propose distributed reasoning solutions considering data distributed over different elements in a AmI system. The main concern of DRAGO is to reason in distributed environments overcoming the barrier of the heterogeneous knowledge representation that independent entities in a AmI system are very likely to employ. As such, DRAGO is only capable of performing ontological reasoning to check concept satisfiability or subsumption. It relies on pre-defined mappings to align different ontologies. In a similar way, P2P-DR and P2PIS are peer-to-peer frameworks in which peers can communicate with a subset of the other available peers to import the knowledge necessary to answer queries based on mappings that define how its local knowledge relates to its peers knowledge. In such way, P2P-DR and P2PIS are capable of performing inference to answer queries that check if a rule is true or false, in which the knowledge, i.e., set of literals that represent context information, is fully distributed in a peer-to-peer system. Nevertheless, P2P-DR and P2PIS are not capable of answering queries with variables. Moreover, DRAGO, P2P-DR and P2PIS are also limited by the fact that in practical implementations of AmI it is not feasible to build in advance mappings of all possible pairs of different ontologies that may be needed. Other techniques capable of dynamically aligning knowledge representations are more adequate in such conditions [6].

After discussing the positive and negative characteristics of the related work, we enumerate in the next section the design strategies for implementing a decentralized reasoning service and present our approach.

References

1. Adjiman, P., Chatalic, P., Goasdoué, F., Rousset, M., Simon, L.: Distributed reasoning in a P2P setting: Application to the semantic web. J. Artif. Intell. Res. (JAIR) **25**, 269–314 (2006)
2. Bikakis, A., Antoniou, G.: Distributed reasoning with conflicts in an ambient peer-to-peer setting. In: Mühlhäuser, M., Ferscha, A., Aitenbichler, E. (eds.) Constructing Ambient Intelligence, Communications in Computer and Information Science, vol. 11 Part 1, pp. 24–33, Springer, Heidelberg (2008). doi:10.1007/978-3-540-85379-4_4
3. Bikakis, A., Antoniou, G.: Distributed defeasible contextual reasoning in ambient computing. In: Proceedings of the European Conference on Ambient Intelligence (AmI '08), pp. 308–325. Springer, Berlin (2008) doi:10.1007/978-3-540-89617-3_20

4. Bikakis, A., Patkos, T., Antoniou, G., Plexousakis, D.: A survey of semantics-based approaches for context reasoning in ambient intelligence. In: Mühlhäuser, M., Ferscha, A., Aitenbichler, E. (eds.) Constructing Ambient Intelligence, Communications in Computer and Information Science, vol. 11 Part 1, pp. 14–23, Springer, Heidelberg (2008). doi:10.1007/978-3-540-85379-4_3

5. Bouquet, P., Giunchiglia, F., van Harmelen, F., Serafini, L., Stuckenschmidt, H.: C-OWL: Contextualizing ontologies. In: Proceedings of the Second International Semantic Web Conference (ISWC-2003), Lecture Notes in Computer Science, vol. 2870, pp. 164–179. Springer, Heidelberg (2003)

6. Breitman, K., Felicíssimo, C., Casanova, M.A.: CATO—A lightweight ontology alignment tool. In: Belo, O., Eder, J., e Cunha, J.F., Pastor, O. (eds.) Short Paper Procedings of the 17th Conference on Advanced Information Systems Engineering (CAiSE '05), vol. 161, pp. 83–88 (2005)

7. Chen, H., Finin, T., Joshi, A.: A context broker for building smart meeting rooms. In: Proceedings of the Knowledge Representation and Ontology for Autonomous Systems Symposium, pp. 53–60. Honolulu, Hawaii (2004)

8. Fielding, R., Taylor, R.: Principled design of the modern web architecture. ACM Trans. Internet Technol. 2(2), 115–150 (2002) doi:10.1145/514183.514185

9. Haarslev, V., Möller, R.: RACER system description. In: Goré, R., Leitsch, A., Nipkow, T. (eds.) Automated Reasoning, Lecture Notes in Computer Science, vol. 2083, pp. 701–705, Springer, Heidelberg (2001). doi:10.1007/3-540-45744-5_59

10. Mrohs, B., Luther, M., Vaidya, R., Wagner, M., Steglich, S., Kellerer, W., Arbanowski, S.: OWL-SF - A distributed semantic service framework. In: Proceedings of Workshop on Context Awareness for Proactive Systems (CAPS), pp. 67–78. Helsinki, Finland (2005)

11. Ranganathan, A., Campbell, R.: A middleware for context-aware agents in ubiquitous computing environments. Lecture Notes Comput. Sci. 2672, 143–161 (2003)

12. Ranganathan, A., Campbell, R.: An infrastructure for context-awareness based on first order logic. Pers. Ubiquit. Comput. 7(6), 353–364 (2003)

13. Román, M., Hess, C., Cerqueira, R., Ranganathan, A., Campbell, R., Nahrstedt, K.: A Middleware infrastructure for active spaces. IEEE Pervasive Comput. 1(4), 74–83 (2002)

14. Sameshima, S., Suzuk, J., Steglich, S., Suda, T.: Platform Independent Model (PIM) and Platform Specific Model (PSM) for Super Distributed Objects. Final adopted specification, Object Management Group. Available at http://www.omg.org/cgi-bin/doc?sdo/03-09-01 (2003)

15. Serafini, L., Tamilin, A.: DRAGO: Distributed Reasoning architecture for the semantic web. In: Gómez-Pérez, A., Euzenat, J. (eds.) ESWC, Lecture Notes in Computer Science, vol. 3532, pp. 361–376. Springer, Heidelberg (2005)

16. Sirin, E., Parsia, B.: Pellet: An OWL DL reasoner. In: Haarslev, V., Möller, R. (eds.) Proceedings of International Workshop on Description Logics, CEUR, vol. 104, CEUR-WS.org, Springer, Heidelberg (2004)

17. Soldatos, J., Dimakis, N., Stamatis, K., Polymenakos, L.: A breadboard architecture for pervasive context-aware services in smart spaces: middleware components and prototype applications. Pers. Ubiquit. Comput. J. 11(3), 193–212 (2007). doi:10.1007/s00779-006-0102-7

18. Wang, X., Dong, J., Chin, C., Hettiarachchi, S., Zhang, D.: Semantic space: an infrastructure for smart spaces. Pervasive Comput. 3(3), 32–39 (2004)

Chapter 4
Cooperative Reasoning

Abstract This chapter presents our proposal of a process to perform decentralized reasoning. In the first section we explain the system model on which we base our proposal, which is formalized and explained in the following sections. Finally, we discuss design strategies to implement the service.

Keywords Ambient Intelligence · Ubiquitous computing · Context-awareness · Rule-based reasoning · Decentralized reasoning · Cooperative reasoning

4.1 System Model

As we discussed in Sect. 2.5, in ubiquitous systems, actions or adaptations are triggered when specific situations take place, for example, a projector may be set up to show a specific set of slides when a speaker enters a conference room to give a presentation [4], or a device may be disconnected from a collaborative presentation session if the user leaves a room [7]. These situations can be described by derivation rules—represented in some type of logic—and hence may be identified by reasoning operations [1].

Most middleware systems for ubiquitous applications support rule-based inference [2], traditionally adopting a centralized approach for their reasoning mechanisms, as we argued in Chap. 3. This is the case of CoBrA [5], CHIL [8] and Semantic Space [9], for example. However, these reasoning operations may need to evaluate context data collected from distributed sources and stored in different devices, as usually not all context data is readily available to all elements of a ubiquitous environment.

In our *system model*, we assumed that there are two main interacting parties in the reasoning process: the *user side* and the *ambient side*, both comprised by the services, applications and data that are available at each side. In fact, not all context information is available both at the users' mobile devices and at the ambient infrastructure.

J. Viterbo and M. Endler, *Decentralized Reasoning in Ambient Intelligence*,
SpringerBriefs in Computer Science, DOI: 10.1007/978-1-4471-4168-6_4,
© The Author(s) 2012

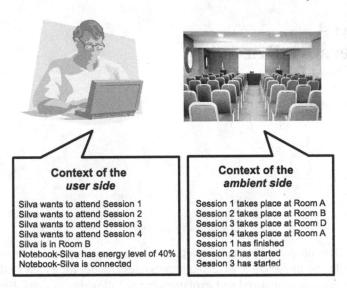

Fig. 4.1 Example of context information that might be available at the user and the ambient sides of our scenario example

For several reasons, ranging from privacy to performance issues, some information may be available only on the *user side*, while some other information may be available only on the *ambient side*. For instance, taking our scenario (c.f. Sect. 2.1), at the *user side* Silva's notebook stores information about his affiliation, subjects of interest, sessions, besides his devices' resources and location. At the *ambient side* the infrastructure stores information about the event and the environment, such as the assignment of rooms and status of each session, the status of devices (e.g., projectors that are turned on), volume of sound in the rooms, etc.

Figure 4.1 shows an example of some context information that might be available on each side at a given moment. Both sides share a common context model, described Sect. 2.4, but have different context information, as will be formalized in Sect. 4.4. In the figure, we can observe that the context data related with a specific predicate, i.e., the ontology facts, are available either on the *user side*, such as "wantsToAttend", or on the *user side*, such as "takesPlace", but never on both sides. This non-overlapping condition is necessary in our two-tier model, to allow the partitioning of rules in the cooperative inference process.

We assume that applications executing on the ambient infrastructure or on the user's device rely on a rule-based reasoning service—provided by the middleware— to identify context-dependent relevant situations. A situation is described using a DL-safe rule R, in which the free variables correspond to individuals that may be available at either side. These applications may query or subscribe at the reasoning service, providing the rule R to be inferred. The result of the reasoning operation is a set of tuples S with individuals that satisfy the rule. We assume that there is no message loss in the communication among the entities in the system.

4.2 Patterns of Interaction

Hence, for a reasoning service—running on either side—to infer relevant situations based on rules provided by applications, we devise three possible patterns of interaction: (a) *user side reasoning*, if the reasoning is performed based only on context information available at the *user side*, (b) *ambient side reasoning*, if the reasoning is performed based only on context information available at the *ambient side*, or (c) *cooperative reasoning*, when the reasoning is performed based on context information stored at both sides.

4.2.1 User Side Reasoning

Applications executing on mobile devices may be interested in situations expressed by rules in which all involved free variables represent context information available at the device. For example, in our scenario, assuming that the ConfComp was configured to warn Silva to recharge notebook when he is waiting between sessions in the lobby of the conference center. The application needs to identify the situation described by Rule 4.1, which involves device's capabilities and the user's location, the desired situation could be inferred solely based on context data available at the device. The rule states that "if Silva is located in the lobby and his mobile device's battery has less than 40% energy, then he should recharge it". In this case a reasoning service executing on the device would be able to check when the rule can be triggered.

Rule 4.1:

$$hasEnergyLevel(\text{"Notebook-Silva"}, ?c) \land lessThan(?c, \text{"40\%"}) \land$$
$$isLocatedIn(\text{"Silva"}, \text{"Lobby"}) \longrightarrow shouldRecharge(\text{"Notebook-Silva"})$$

4.2.2 Ambient Side Reasoning

If all context data necessary to find the result for a rule is available to the ambient infrastructure's services, the reasoning operation can be performed entirely at the ambient side. Revisiting our scenario, let us assume that an application at the ambient side is interested in the situation described by Rule 4.2, which states that "if a conference session takes place in a given room and the session has already started, then the room is busy". In this case a reasoning service running on the ambient infrastructure would be able to infer the rule.

Rule 4.2:

$$takesPlace(?s, ?r) \land hasStarted(?s) \longrightarrow isBusy(?r)$$

4.2.3 Cooperative Reasoning

As a third possibility, a situation may be described by a rule containing context variables that refer to context information available both at the devices and at the ambient infrastructure. For instance, taking Rule 4.3, which states that "if Silva is located in a room where a conference session is supposed to take place and this session has already started, then Silva is busy". As shown in Fig. 4.1, the user's location data is available only at the user side, while the information about the sessions is available only at the ambient side.

Rule 4.3:

$isLocatedIn("Silva", ?r) \land takesPlace(?s, ?r) \land hasStarted(?s) \longrightarrow isBusy("Silva")$

In this case, for a reasoning service executing in the ambient infrastructure to be able to infer the rule, it would have to collect and store all context data produced in that environment—both by the ambient infrastructure itself and by all the users' devices—in a centralized way. Although there are usually no computational limitations for the ambient infrastructure related to storing or processing the large amounts of context data necessary for such reasoning, privacy issues may prevent the user from accepting the disclosure of his personal information—such as his location or personal preferences—to the ambient infrastructure.

As an option, the device at the *user side* could collect and store all context information available at the *ambient side* that would be necessary for reasoning about the proposed rules. To follow this approach, however, would entail another problem: the reasoning computation may be too heavy to be performed by the resource-limited mobile device. In fact, we can only expect that inference operations be efficiently executed on a mobile device when the corresponding rules refer exclusively to context information available at the device, rather than provided by the ambient.

We conclude that, for such types of rules, reasoning should neither be performed solely by the device, nor by the ambient infrastructure. It should rather be executed involving reasoning services on both sides, performing what we define as "cooperative reasoning". In the cooperative reasoning each side should be in charge of analyzing the context information available locally, then the outcomes of each side would have to be combined to produce an appropriate result. For this purpose, however, a strategy for cooperating in the reasoning operation needs to be defined.

4.3 Design Strategies for a Reasoning Service

In Chap. 3 we discussed the main characteristics of several reasoning approaches for distributed scenarios. We noticed that these approaches either are not completely distributed, or are not capable of inferring complex rules with variables, indicating that there must be a balance between these features. As such, in Sect. 4.1 we proposed our system model, which is not completely distributed, characterizing AmI systems as a two-tier model. In the previous section we discussed all possible patterns of interaction for reasoning based on this model. Bearing in mind the main functionalities of the related work and the characteristics of our model, we now discuss the functional and non-functional attributes that compose the design strategies for implementing a service to perform decentralized reasoning.

4.3.1 Functional Attributes

D1. Support to Rule-Based Reasoning:

As a first design strategy we identify the need for the service to perform inference based on rules. Rules provide not only a formal model to describe situations of interest, but also a general-purpose representation of particular combinations of context data that are relevant for ubiquitous applications or services.

D2. Use of Variables:

Free variables in rules give more flexibility to the description of situations, as the developer can refer generically to the elements of a domain, rather than mention each specifically. The result of the reasoning operation for such a rule is a set of tuples representing individuals in the ABox that bind to the variables mentioned in the consequent of the rule, like in database queries. This, however, imposes a greater complexity on the implementation of the service.

D3. Support to Decentralized Reasoning:

The reasoning service must be able to infer situations described by rules that depend on decentralized context data, i.e., context information that is distributed at the different parties of our model: the *user side* and the *ambient side*. For reasons ranging from privacy to inference performance, it may be the case that neither side has access to full context information.

D3.1. Support to Local Reasoning:

As discussed in Sects. 4.2.1 and 4.2.2, when all necessary context data is available at the reasoning side, the reasoning may be performed locally, i.e., inferred in local reasoning.

D3.2. Support to Cooperative Reasoning:

On the other hand, as discussed in Sect. 4.2.3, there should be support for *cooperative reasoning*, i.e., where services both at the *user side* and the *ambient side* are in charge of analyzing the context information available locally, and having the outcomes of each entities' local reasoning combined to determine the global inference result.

D4. Support to Synchronous Queries:

The reasoning service must be able to evaluate a rule and respond immediately to a query submitted by a client application. In case of *cooperative reasoning*, the peer reasoners have to be able to interact to produce an immediate response to the client application, as will be explained in Sect. 5.1.1. This is necessary for applications that need to check if a given situation is satisfied, e.g., "is there some event scheduled for this room I am entering?"

D5. Support to Asynchronous Communication:

This functionality is important because, due to the intrinsic limitation imposed by query-only reasoning, a client requiring up-to-date information about a situation would have to continuously poll the reasoner, causing higher load to the service and network, and draining the already scarce resources of mobile devices [6]. On the other hand, in the publish/subscribe approach the client is notified as soon as the rule is triggered, allowing a timely response of the system for the situation of interest. In the case of *cooperative reasoning*, the peer reasoners have to be able to interact to determine the result for the reasoning operation for a rule submitted by a client application each time its result changes, until this application removes the rule. This strategy will be discussed in Sect. 5.1.1.

4.3.2 Non-Functional Attributes

D6. Scalability:

The decentralized reasoning service must be able to work efficiently in scenarios where a great number of users—through their mobile devices—interact with the ambient services. In such environments, many interests of client applications request the reasoning services, which have to be able to manage a great mumber of subscriptions with different rules.

D7. Response Time:

The reasoning service must be able to detect/infer situations shortly after they take place, i.e., after the context variables assume values that satisfy a rule. In particular, the latency between a context data change and its corresponding notification to the client applications must be sufficiently small for triggering the adaptations specific of that scenario.

D8. Communication Traffic:

The communication traffic involving the decentralized reasoners must not deteriorate the overall communication quality of the system.

D9. Memory Consumption:

The memory footprint of the reasoning service must be such that it can be executed on any device used in the ubiquitous system.

D10. Robustness and Resilience:

The reasoning service must be able to work correctly despite some failures of the underlying infrastructure. For that sake, the service must be able to deal with failures in the communication between the client application and the reasoner or between the different parts of the reasoner, such as message loss or content error.

D11. Portability:

As a part of the decentralized service has to be executed on the ambient infrastructure, and the other part on the users' mobile devices, the service implementation should be easily portable to different mobile or fixed devices.

In this work, we focus on two main non-functional attributes, response time (D7) and communication traffic (D8). The other attributes will be further tackled in future work. Before presenting our proposal of a reasoning process that meets the design strategies discussed above, in the following section we formalize the cooperative reasoning operation to be able to draw an adequate strategy that solves this problem.

4.4 Cooperative Reasoning Formalization

Initially, let us assume that our domain $\mathcal{D}$ is described in a knowledge base comprised by a TBox $\mathcal{T}$, which defines all the unary and binary predicates $P \in \mathcal{P}$, i.e., classes and properties that are used to describe that domain, and an ABox $\mathcal{A}$, containing all the named individuals $I \in \mathcal{I}$ and all the asserted facts $F \in \mathcal{F}$ that represent the context data of that domain.

A rule R, decidable in $\mathcal{D}$, is composed by an antecedent R_{ant} and a consequent R_{con}, and represented as $R : R_{ant} \rightarrow R_{con}$. The antecedent R_{ant} consists of a conjunction of atoms, each in the form $P(x)$, representing an unary assertion, or in the form $P(x, y)$, representing a binary assertion, such that $P \in \mathcal{P}$, i.e., P is a predicate valid in that domain, and x and y are either individuals $I \in \mathcal{I}$ or free variables that represent such individuals.

The consequent R_{con} corresponds to an atom either in the form $P_c(x_c)$, representing an unary assertion, or in the form $P_c(x_c, y_c)$, representing a binary assertion, where P_c is a new predicate to be inferred, and x_c and y_c are either individuals defined in $\mathcal{A}$ or free variables that represent such individuals. All free variables in R_{con} must appear also in R_{ant}. This rule is represented in the Eq. 4.1:

$$R : \wedge P(x[, y]) \longrightarrow P_c(x_c[, y_c]) \tag{4.1}$$

The result of the reasoning operation—or inference—for the rule R is a set S of tuples that represent bindings for the free variables appearing in R_{con}. The first step of the inference consists in finding a set T containing all tuples t that represent valid bindings for the free variables in R_{ant}, i.e., tuples of individuals $I \in \mathcal{I}$ that replacing each variable in R_{ant}, make it a true proposition, with each atom corresponding to a fact $F \in \mathcal{F}$. In the second step, as each free variable in R_{con} corresponds to a free variable in R_{ant}, each tuple $t \in T$ yields a tuple $s \in S$.

As an example, let us consider a TBox that defines the unary predicates P_a and P_b and the binary predicates P_c and P_d, and an ABox that contains the individuals I_1, I_2, I_3, I_4, I_5 and I_6, and the facts $P_a(I_1), P_a(I_2), P_a(I_3), P_b(I_4), P_b(I_5), P_b(I_6)$, $P_c(I_1, I_3), P_c(I_1, I_4), P_c(I_2, I_5), P_d(I_1, I_5), P_d(I_2, I_6)$, and the rule R_1 as follows:

$$R_1 : P_a(x) \bigwedge P_c(x, y) \wedge P_d(x, z) \longrightarrow P_{con}(y, z) \tag{4.2}$$

The result S for this reasoning operation is determined by finding the set T of all tuples t with possible values for the variables x, y and z, selected in $\{I_1, I_2, I_3, I_4, I_5, I_6\}$, such that when we replace the variables in R_{ant} by the values in a tuple t, each atom will correspond to a fact $F \in \mathcal{F}$. For example, if we pick the tuple $t = (I_1, I_4, I_5)$ and replace x, y and z in R, we have:

$$P_a(I_1) \wedge P_c(I_1, I_4) \wedge P_d(I_1, I_5) \longrightarrow P_f(I_4, I_5). \tag{4.3}$$

In this case, each atom in R_{ant} corresponds to a fact in the ABox, as such $t \in T$ represents a valid tuple, yielding the tuple $s = (I_4, I_5) \in S$ as one of the solutions for the rule, i.e., we can infer the fact $P_f(I_4, I_5)$ from R_1. The complete set T is $T = \{(I_1, I_3, I_5), (I_1, I_4, I_5), (I_2, I_5, I_6)\}$, and the result S for the inference of R_1 is $S = \{(I_3, I_5), (I_4, I_5), (I_5, I_6)\}$.

Let us now consider our two-tier scenario, where the context data is distributed over two different sides, one representing the *user side* and the other representing the *ambient side*. As such, our domain $\mathcal{D}'$ needs to be described as the integration of the two knowledge bases (ontologies) [3]: a local knowledge base $\mathcal{D}_L = \{\mathcal{T}_L, \mathcal{A}_L\}$, representing the local context information, i.e., on the side where we start the inference of a rule, and a remote knowledge base $\mathcal{D}_R = \{\mathcal{T}_R, \mathcal{A}_R\}$, representing the remote context information. The overall TBox $\mathcal{T}'$ consists in the integration of $\mathcal{T}_L$ and $\mathcal{T}_R$, which define the set of local predicates $\mathcal{P}_L$ and the set of remote predicates $\mathcal{P}_R$, respectively. The overall ABox $\mathcal{A}'$ consists in the integration of $\mathcal{A}_L$, containing the set of named individuals $\mathcal{I}_L$ and the set of asserted facts $\mathcal{F}_L$ that represent the local context information, and $\mathcal{A}_R$, containing the set of named individuals $\mathcal{I}_R$ and the set of asserted facts $\mathcal{F}_R$ that represent the context information on the remote side. In our model, where predicates and facts are associated with context providers and the respective provided information, the local and remote side do not share these elements, such that $\mathcal{P}_L \cap \mathcal{P}_R = \emptyset$ and $\mathcal{F}_L \cap \mathcal{F}_R = \emptyset$. On the other hand, some individuals may be present on both sides, such that $\mathcal{I}_L \cap \mathcal{I}_R \neq \emptyset$.

Given a rule $R' : R_{ant} \longrightarrow R_{con}$, decidable in $\mathcal{D}'$, the antecedent R_{ant} consists in the conjunction of atoms in the form $P(x)$ or $P(x, y)$, such that $P \in \mathcal{P}_L$ or $P \in \mathcal{P}_R$, and x and y may be individuals $I \in \mathcal{I}_L \bigcup \mathcal{I}_L$ or free variables that represent these individuals. We can rewrite R_{ant} as the conjunction of two parts, a local part R_L, containing all the atoms of R_{ant} where $P \in \mathcal{P}_L$, and a remote part R_R, containing all the atoms of R_{ant} where $P \in \mathcal{P}_R$, such that R' may be represented as in the Eq. 4.4:

$$R' : R_L \wedge R_R \longrightarrow P_c(x_c[, y_c]), \quad \text{where } R_L = \wedge P_L(x[, y]) \quad \text{and}$$
$$R_R = \wedge P_R(x[, y]) \tag{4.4}$$

In the *cooperative reasoning*, we want to reason about R' without performing an integration of the local and remote knowledge bases. As such, R_L and R_R have to be evaluated separately, in different—but complementary—operations. First, in the *local reasoning* we find a set T_L of tuples t_L that represent valid bindings for the free variables in R_L, i.e., individuals $I \in \mathcal{I}_L$ that replacing the variables in R_L will make each atom correspond to a fact $F \in \mathcal{F}_L$. As R_L may have some variables in common with R_R, which we will define as the set V, this partial result bounds the next reasoning operation. In the *remote reasoning* we will have to find a set T_R of tuples t_R representing valid bindings for the variables in R_R, such that each tuple t_R has the same values for all variables $v \in V$ that appear in at least one tuple $t_L \in T_L$. Each pair t_L and t_R in which the variables $v \in V$ have the same value is a correlated pair, and the final set T of bindings for the all free variables in R_{ant} corresponds to the combination (merge) of each correlated pair. Finally, each tuple $t \in T$ yields a tuple $s \in S$.

For example, let us consider a local side where a TBox defines the unary predicate P_a and binary predicates P_c, and an ABox contains the individuals $I_1, I_2, I_3, I_4, I_5, I_6$ and I_7, and the facts $P_a(I_1), P_a(I_3), P_c(I_1, I_4), P_c(I_1, I_5), P_c(I_2, I_6)$ and $P_c(I_3, I_7)$, and a remote side where a TBox defines the unary predicate P_b and the binary predicate P_d, and an ABox contains the individuals $I_1, I_2, I_3, I_8, I_9, I_{10}$ and I_{11}, and the facts $P_b(I_8), P_b(I_9), P_b(I_{10}), P_d(I_1, I_8), P_d(I_1, I_9), P_d(I_1, I_{11}), P_d(I_2, I_8)$ and $P_d(I_3, I_{10})$, and the rule R_2 as follows:

$$R_2 : P_a(x) \wedge P_b(z) \wedge P_c(x, y) \wedge P_d(x, z) \longrightarrow P_f(y, z) \qquad (4.5)$$

The local part of this rule is $R_L = P_a(x) \wedge P_c(x, y)$. First, in the *local reasoning*, we had to find the set T_L of all tuples t_L with values for (x, y) that satisfied R_L, which corresponds to $T_L = \{(I_1, I_4), (I_1, I_5), (I_3, I_7)\}$. The remote part of the rule is $R_R = P_b(z) \wedge P_d(x, z)$. As x is a variable common in R_L and R_R, in the *remote reasoning* we had to find the set T_R of all tuples t_R with values for (x, z) that satisfied R_L and had $x = I_1$ or $x = I_3$, which corresponds to $T_R = \{(I_1, I_8), (I_1, I_9), (I_3, I_{10})\}$. Combining the partial results we found $T = \{(I_1, I_4, I_8), (I_1, I_5, I_8), (I_1, I_4, I_9), (I_1, I_5, I_9), (I_3, I_7, I_{10})\}$, yielding the result $S = \{(I_4, I_8), (I_5, I_8), (I_4, I_9), (I_5, I_9), (I_7, I_{10})\}$. Below, we selected the tuple $(I_1, I_4, I_9) \in T$ to rewrite R_2, replacing the variables x, y and z, and show that the tuple $(I_4, I_9) \in S$ is a possible result, i.e., is one of the facts inferred by R_2, as all atoms of R_{ant} are facts $F \in \mathcal{F}_L \bigcup \mathcal{F}_R$.

$$P_a(I_1) \wedge P_b(I_9) \wedge P_c(I_1, I_4) \wedge P_d(I_1, I_9) \longrightarrow P_f(I_4, I_9) \qquad (4.6)$$

Summarizing, the *cooperative reasoning* it consists in:

1. Splitting the antecedent of the rule in a *local part* and a *remote part*;
2. Performing the reasoning about the *local part* of the rule in the local knowledge base to find a preliminary result T;
3. Performing the reasoning about the *remote part* of the rule in the remote knowledge base, bounded by the preliminary result; and
4. Combine the partial results to obtain the final result S.

In the next section we propose a strategy to perform this operation as distributed algorithm in which two reasoners cooperate exchanging messages that contain the information needed.

4.5 Discussion

In this chapter, we described the possible patterns of interaction in a system where not all context information is available for the entity in charge of performing the reasoning operation. We also discussed the functional and non-functional attributes that compose the design strategies for implementing a rule-based reasoner to be executed in such scenario. After that we formalized the *cooperative reasoning* operation. In the next chapter we propose a strategy to execute this reasoning operation and describe the distributed algorithm and communication protocol necessary to perform the complete *cooperative reasoning process*.

References

1. Anagnostopoulos, C.B., Ntarladimas, Y., Hadjiefthymiades, S.: Situational computing: An innovative architecture with imprecise reasoning. J. Syst. Softw. **80**(12), 1993–2014 (2007). doi:10.1016/j.jss.2007.03.003
2. Bikakis, A., Patkos, T., Antoniou, G., Plexousakis, D.: A survey of semantics-based approaches for context reasoning in ambient intelligence. In: Bergmann, R., Althoff, K.D., Furbach, U., Schmid, K. (eds.) Proceedings of the Workshop Artificial Intelligence Methods for Ambient Intelligence at the European Conference on Ambient Intelligence (AmI'07), pp. 15–24. Springer, New York (2007)
3. Cafezeiro, I., Viterbo, J., Rademaker, A., Haeusler, E., Endler, M.: A formal framework for modeling context-aware behavior in ubiquitous computing. In: Proceedings of the 3rd International Symposium on Leveraging Applications of Formal Methods, Verification and Validation (ISoLA 2008), pp. 519–533. Springer, New York (2008)
4. Chen, H., Finin, T., Joshi, A.: An ontology for context-aware pervasive computing environments. Knowl Eng Rev. **18**(3), 197–207 (2003) Special Issue on Ontologies for Distributed Systems
5. Chen, H., Finin, T., Joshi, A.: A context broker for building smart meeting rooms. In: Proceedings of the Knowledge Representation and Ontology for Autonomous Systems Symposium, pp. 53–60. Honolulu, Hawaii (2004)
6. Cugola, G., Jacobsen, H.A.: Using publish/subscribe middleware for mobile systems. ACM SIGMOBILE Mobile Comput. Commun. Rev. **6**(4), 25–33 (2002). doi:10.1145/643550.643552
7. Malcher, M.A., Endler, M.: A context-aware collaborative presentation system for handhelds. In: Proceedings of the 5th Brazilian Symposium of Collaborative Systems (SBSC 2008), pp. 1–11 (2008). IEEE Computer Society, Los Alamitos, CA, USA
8. Soldatos, J., Dimakis, N., Stamatis, K., Polymenakos, L.: A breadboard architecture for pervasive context-aware services in smart spaces: middleware components and prototype applications. Pers. Ubiquit Comput. J. **11**(3), 193–212 (2007). doi:10.1007/s00779-006-0102-7
9. Wang, X., Dong, J., Chin, C., Hettiarachchi, S., Zhang, D.: Semantic space: an infrastructure for smart spaces. Pervasive Comput. **3**(3), 32–39 (2004)

Chapter 5
Our Approach for Cooperative Reasoning

Abstract This chapter presents our proposal of an algorithm and protocol that implement the *cooperative reasoning process*, according with the design strategies discussed in the last chapter.

Keywords Ambient Intelligence · Ubiquitous computing · Context-awareness · Rule-based reasoning · Decentralized reasoning · Cooperative reasoning · Distributed algorithm

5.1 Strategy for Rule-Based Context Reasoning

We propose a strategy in which two entities—a reasoner running on the user side, the *device reasoner*, and another one running on the ambient side, the *ambient reasoner*—interact to infer situations described by rules involving context variables depending on data collected from different sources and stored at both sides, performing what we defined as *cooperative reasoning*.

Each of these entities (called *cooperative reasoners*) aggregate context information obtained from local context providers available at each side and execute the reasoning of rules submitted by applications running on either side. As the interaction may start at the *ambient side* or at the *user side*, depending on which side the client application is running, we call *local reasoner* the one executing at the side where the interaction begins, and *remote reasoner* the other one.

Depending on the rule to be inferred, the reasoning operation may follow one of the patterns presented in Sect. 4.2: user side, ambient side or cooperative reasoning. Now we describe the cooperative reasoning process for a rule R, submitted to the reasoning service by a client application, highlighting each step of the process, and hence defining our proposed cooperative reasoning strategy. As discussed in Sect. 4.3, the client application may query the reasoner to get an immediate response about a submitted rule R or may subscribe to be notified whenever the situation described by

Fig. 5.1 Box diagram representing the cooperative reasoning strategy for a synchronous query

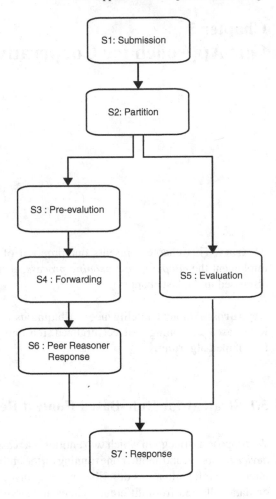

R holds. As such, this cooperation can have two different general forms of interaction, the synchronous and the asynchronous interactions.

Figures 5.1 and 5.2 show box diagrams in which each of the thirteen steps of our strategy are represented. We divided these steps into two different groups, the synchronous interaction steps and the asynchronous interaction steps, which we describe, in more detail, as follows.

5.1.1 Synchronous Interaction

The synchronous interaction starts when a client application submits a *synchronous query* to the *local reasoner*, as described in the following paragraphs.

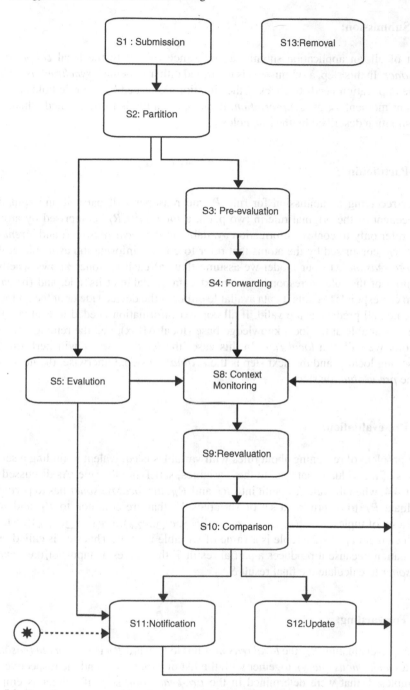

Fig. 5.2 Box diagram representing the cooperative reasoning strategy for an asynchronous interaction

S1. Submission:

First of all, an application submits an inference rule R to the local *cooperative reasoner*. In this step, a submission is identified either as being a *synchronous query*, if the application needs to check if the situation described by the rule holds at that current moment, or as a *subscription*, if the application is to be notified whenever the situation described by the rule holds.

S2. Partitioning:

After receiving a submission for rule R, the reasoner will parse it and split the antecedent of the original rule in two parts, a *local part* R_L, comprised by atoms that refer only to context information available at the *local reasoner*, and a *remote part* R_R, comprised by the atoms that refer to context information available at the *remote reasoner*. In our model we assume that (a) each reasoner knows whether an atom of the rule corresponds to context data available at its side, and (b) each atom corresponds to context data available either at the device side or at the ambient side, i.e., all predicates are valid. If all context information needed to evaluate the rule is available at the local knowledge base (local ABox), i.e., the remote part R_R is void, we call R a *local rule*. In this case, the *local reasoner* will perform the reasoning locally, and the next step is the *evaluation* step. Otherwise, the next step is the *pre-evaluation* step.

S3. Pre-evaluation:

The problem of reasoning about rules with variables is equivalent to finding a set of tuples of individuals that bind to that variables, satisfying the rule. As discussed in Sect. 4.4, when the rule R is split into R_L and R_R, the *local reasoner* has to partially evaluate R_L to determine a set of variables V, that are common to R_L and R_R, and a set of tuples $T = \{(c_{1,1}, c_{1,2}..c_{1,n}), (c_{2,1}, c_{2,2}..c_{2,n})..(c_{k,1}, c_{k,2}..c_{k,n})\}$, where each element $c_{i,j}$ of the tuple is a value of variable $v_j \in V$. This step is called pre-evaluation because it produces a partial result T that serves as input for the *remote reasoner* to calculate the final result S.

S4. Forwarding:

After pre-evaluating R_L, the *local reasoner* has to forward R_R to the *remote reasoner* (as a *synchronous query*), together with the list of variables V and the respective set of tuples T that were determined in the *pre-evaluation* step, if neither is empty. The *local reasoner* will wait for the response from the *remote reasoner* in the *peer reasoner response* step.

S5. Evaluation:

This step consists in performing the reasoning operation over the context data available locally to get the set of tuples S, corresponding to the tuples of individuals that satisfy the *local rule*. A rule that was forwarded by the other reasoner is also dealt in this step. In this case, for obtaining S the reasoner evaluates the rule bounded by the set of tuples T, containing the possible values for the set of variables in V. The next step is the *response* step.

S6. Peer Reasoner Response:

When the rule is not local, it will be partitioned and have the *remote part* R_R evaluated by the *remote reasoner*, according with the pre-condition imposed by the set of variables V and the set of tuples T associated, as described in Step S5. After forwarding R_R (Step S3), the *local reasoner* will wait for the response from the *remote reasoner* containing the set of tuples S that corresponds to the result, going to the following step.

S7. Response:

The result obtained for a *local rule* will be sent to the application client immediately after the *evaluation* (Step S5). For a rule that is not local, the *local reasoner* will go through Steps S3 and S4, and after that it will wait for the response from the *remote reasoner* (Step S6) and send to the application client the set of tuples S, received from the *remote reasoner*.

5.1.2 Asynchronous Interaction

The asynchronous interaction starts when a client application submits a rule R to the *local reasoner* as a *subscription*. The initial steps (S1 to S5) are very similar to what was described for the synchronous interaction in Sect. 5.1.1. After the rule R is submitted (Step S1), it is partitioned (Step S2), and if it is not a *local rule*, it goes through the *pre-evaluation* (Step S3) and the *forwarding* (Step S4), but as a subscription. After that, however, the reasoner goes to the *context monitoring* step (Step S8). On the other hand, if the submitted rule R is local, after the *partitioning* (Step S2) the next step will be the *evaluation* (Step S5) and after that the *notification* (Step S11) or *the context monitoring* (Step S8), as indicated in Fig. 5.2. The Steps S8 to S13 in the asynchronous interaction are presented in the following paragraphs.

S8. Context Monitoring:

After the first evaluation of a *local rule* (Step S5), or after the *remote part* R_R of a rule is forwarded to the *remote reasoner*, each *subscription* is put into a list of subscriptions with the associated data. This comprises the information about the client application that submitted the subscription, the *local part* and *remote part* (if it exists) of the rule, the sets of free variables V and tuples T that were sent to the *remote reasoner* (or received from a *local reasoner*, in case the reasoning plays the role of the *remote reasoner* and R corresponds to a *forwarded rule*). Each time there is a change in context data that may affect one of the rules in the list, each of these rules is selected so that the reasoner can perform a *reevaluation* of the rule (Step S9).

S9. Reevaluation:

After a change in context data that may affect a rule associated with a *subscription*, if the rule is a *local rule*, the reasoner checks the rule performing a new reasoning operation to find a set of tuples of individuals S that satisfy the rule. If the rule is not local, similarly to what was described in Step S3 of the synchronous interaction, R_L will be evaluated to find an updated set of tuples T with values for each variable in V that are common in R_L and R_R. In Step 10, the results of this step are compared with the ones that were previously obtained.

S10. Comparison:

The sets of tuples S or T, which were determined in the *reevaluation* step, are compared with sets of tuples previously found. If there are no differences between the sets, no action will be taken and the process returns to (Step S8). Otherwise, the reasoner will store the new results for future comparisons. If the rule is a *local rule*, the reasoner will proceed to the *notification* step (Step S11). Otherwise, it will proceed to the *update* step (Step S12), which will be explained ahead.

S11. Notification:

A notification for a client may be originated in several forms. (i) After the submission of a rule R (Step S1), if its is partitioned and identified as a *local rule* (Step S2), and in its evaluation (Step S5), a set of tuples of values S that satisfy the rule is found, the *local reasoner* sends this result to the client application as a notification. (ii) From then on, this rule will be monitored (Step S8), reevaluated when necessary (Step S9), and every time a new set S is found, i.e., different from the previous result (Step S10), the client will again be notified. (iii) For rules that had the *remote part* R_R forwarded to the *remote reasoner* (Step S4), upon being received there, R_R goes straight to the evaluation step (Step S5), and may generate a notification in the same way described in *i* and *ii*, but targeting the peer reasoner. On receiving this notification (as indicated by the dashed arrow in Fig. 5.2), the *local reasoner* sends the received result S to the client application, but only if it meets the conditions that will be discussed in Sect. 5.1.3.

S12. Update:

A particular situation may occur if a rule R has a *local part* R_L that is being monitored by the *local reasoner*, and a *remote part* R_R, that was forwarded to the *remote reasoner*. While R_R is being monitored by the *remote reasoner*, changes in the context data may happen also at the local side, which may cause a change in the set of tuples T that were initially determined by the *local reasoner* in the pre-evaluation of R_L (Step S3) and previously forwarded to the *remote reasoner* (Step S4). Therefore, in Step S8 the *local reasoner* monitors the context variables present in the local part R_L of a rule, reevaluates the rule when necessary (Step S9), and updates this information at the *remote reasoner* whenever a new set of tuples T is found. This update is identified by an "update number", that will be used to guarantee that a notification from the *remote reasoner* gives a valid result, as will discussed in Sect. 5.1.3.

S13. Removal:

At any time the client application can remove a subscription. If it corresponds to a *local rule*, the *local reasoner* simply removes it from the list of subscriptions. Otherwise, the *local reasoner* also requests for the *remote reasoner* to remove the part of the rule that was forwarded.

5.1.3 Stability of Context Data

A notification from the *remote reasoner* to the *local reasoner* about the result of a *forwarded rule*, is based on the context data available at the *remote reasoner* at the moment it was generated, and the latest set of tuples T received from the *local reasoner*. This set is first determined in Step S3 and may be subsequently reevaluated in Step S9. Before the notification from the *remote reasoner* arrives at the *local reasoner*, however, there may have been a context data change at the *local reasoner*, which caused a new update to be sent to the *remote reasoner*. In this case, the result S received from the *remote reasoner* can not be considered valid, because it is based on a set of tuples T that has changed.

To prevent the *local reasoner* from sending to the client application a result that is inaccurate, each time a new update is generated by the *local reasoner*, it receives an *update number*, which is sent to the *remote reasoner* together with the new set of tuples T. When the *remote reasoner* finds a set of values S that satisfy a rule, it notifies the *local reasoner*, sending the result S, together with the *update number* of the latest update it received, allowing the local reasoner to check if the result corresponds to the latest update. In Step S11, the *local reasoner*, after receiving this notification, will send the received result S to the client application only if the number of the last update received by the *remote reasoner* matches the number of the last update sent by the *local reasoner*. Otherwise, the result received from the *remote reasoner* will be ignored.

If there are frequent changes of the context data related with a rule R at the *local reasoner*, the reasoners might never converge to find a response and notify the client application. This means that this strategy is not adequate for reasoning with context data that are highly variable. The minimum time t_{reason} that the reasoners take to find a result comprises the periods of time needed for:

1. R_L to be evaluated (or reevaluated) at the *local reasoner*;
2. T to be updated at the *remote reasoner*;
3. R_R to be reevaluated by the *remote reasoner*, finding a result S;
4. the *local reasoner* to receive the notification from the *remote reasoner*;

Let us assume that these changes of the context data occur with mean periodicity of time t_{change}. The necessary condition for guaranteeing the convergence of the inference process is that the context data is stable, i.e., that $t_{change} \gg t_{reason}$. As the *performace* attribute identified in Sect. 4.3 indicates that t_{reason} should be adequate, it is directly related with stability of context data.

5.2 Algorithm

In Sect. 5.1 we described all the general steps that have to be executed to perform a *cooperative reasoning* process. From this description, we can identify that the events that trigger the actions in this process are:

- in a synchronous interaction:

  - the arrival of a new (or forwarded) query;

- in an asynchronous interaction:

  - the arrival of a new (or forwarded) subscription;
  - a change in context data that is being monitored.
  - the arrival of an update from the peer reasoner;
  - the arrival of a notification from the peer reasoner;
  - the removal of a subscription;

In this section we describe the distributed algorithm used to implement a service that performs the proposed process. In fact, the overall process may be divided in blocks of procedures, each triggered by one of the previously mentioned events.

Algorithm 5.1: ON RECEIVING A NEW QUERY

input: A rule R submitted to the reasoner by client C.

1 Partitions R to obtain R_L and R_R
2 **if** $R_R \neq \emptyset$ **then**
3   Pre-evaluates R_L to obtain V and T
4   Forwards R_R, V and T to the remote reasoner
5   Receives S from remote reasoner
6 **end**
7 **else**
8   Evaluates R to obtain S
9 **end**
10 Sends the result S to client C

Algorithm 5.1 shows the code that deals with the synchronous interaction, which is triggered by the arrival of a new or forwarded query. After submission, the rule is partitioned (Line 1), and if it has a *remote part*, it is pre-evaluated to obtain the set of tuples T that is forwarded to the *remote reasoner* together with the list of common variables V (Lines 3 and 4). The *local reasoner* then waits for the reply from the *remote reasoner*, which contains the set of tuples S representing the result for the cooperative reasoning (Line 5). In contrast, if R is a *local rule*, it is immediately evaluated to obtain the set of tuples S that represent the result of the reasoning (Line 8). In either case, the result S is sent to the application client (Line 10). A *forwarded rule* is regarded by the *remote reasoner* in the same form as a *local rule*, and hence is also evaluated (Line 8), generating a response to the *local reasoner* (Line 10).

Algorithm 5.2: ON RECEIVING A NEW SUBSCRIPTION

input: A rule R submitted by client C.

1 Partitions R to obtain R_L and R_R
2 **if** $R_R \neq \emptyset$ **then**
3   Pre-evaluates R_L to obtain V and T
4   Forwards R_R, V and T to the remote reasoner
5 **end**
6 **else**
7   Evaluates R to obtain S
8   **if** $S \neq \emptyset$ **then**
9   Notifies the client C with the result S
10   **end**
11 **end**
12 Puts R_L in list L

Algorithm 5.2 implements the procedure triggered by the arrival of a new subscription from a client, which initiates an asynchronous interaction. As in the synchronous interaction, after the submission, the rule R is partitioned to obtain the *local part* R_L and the *remote part* R_R (Line 1). If R has a remote part R_L, it is pre-evaluated to obtain the set of tuples T (Line 3), which is forwarded to the *remote reasoner* as a subscription, together with the list of common variables V (Line 4). If R is a *local rule*, it is evaluated to obtain the set of tuples S that represents the result of the reasoning (Line 7). If this result is not empty, the client application is notified about the result S. As in the synchronous interaction, a *forwarded rule* is regarded by the *remote reasoner* as a *local rule* that is evaluated (Line 7), possibly generating a notification to the *local reasoner* (Line 9). In either case, the rule is put in a list of subscriptions so that it can be checked whenever an event that may change the result occurs, such as a change in context data, the arrival of an update message from the *local reasoner*, or the arrival of a notification from the *remote reasoner*.

Algorithm 5.3: ON CONTEXT UPDATE

---

input: A change in context data D.

1 **for** *each $R \in L$ affected by D* **do**
2   **if** $R_R = \emptyset$ **then**
3   Reevaluates R_L to obtain S
4   Compares S and *LastResult*
5   **if** $S \neq LastResult$ **then**
6   Stores S as *LastResult*
7   Notifies client C with S [and *LastUpdateNumber*]
8   **end**
9   **end**
10   **else**
11   Reevaluates R_L to obtain T
12   Compares T and $<$
13   **if** $T \neq <$ **then**
14   Stores T as $<$
15   Increments *LastUpdateNumber*
16   Updates R_R, T and *LastUpdateNumber* at the remote reasoner
17   **end**
18   **end**
19 **end**

Each reasoner monitors its local context data (*context monitoring* step), and, as shown in Algorithm 5.3, whenever a change in context is perceived, the list of subscriptions L is checked to select any rule R that may have been affected by the change (Line 1), i.e., rules whose any atom is a predicate related with that context fact. If R is a *local rule*, it is reevaluated to obtain a new set of tuples S (Line 3). The new result S is compared with the previous one stored *LastResult*. If they differ from each other (Lines 4 and 5), the new result is stored as *LastResult* (Line 6) and sent to the client C as a notification (Line 7). If the client C is the peer reasoner, i.e., the rule being monitored corresponds to a *remote part* received from that reasoner, then this notification must include as parameter the number of the last update received from it, $LastUpdateNumber$. If R has a *remote part*, it is reevaluated to obtain a new set of tuples T (Line 11). The new set of tuples T is compared with the last one stored $LastTuples$ and if they are different from each other (Lines 12 and 13), this set of tuples is stored as $LastTuples$ (Line 14) and sent to the *remote reasoner* as an update (Line 16). In this case, a variable $UpdateNumber$ is incremented to identify the number of this update (Line 15) and sent together with T and V.

Algorithm 5.4: ON RECEIVING UPDATE FROM PEER

---

input: An update for rule R containing a set of tuples T and an update number n.

1 Stores n as $LastUpdateNumber$
2 Reevaluates R to obtain S given T
3 Compares S $LastResult$
4 **if** $S \neq LastResult$ **then**
5   Stores S as $LastResult$
6   Notifies the local reasoner with S and $LastUpdateNumber$
7 **end**

As discussed in Step 12 of Sect. 5.1.2, changes in context data at the *local side* may cause a change of the variable values that were previously forwarded to the *remote reasoner*. In this case, the *local reasoner* sends an update to the *remote reasoner* as described in Algorithm 5.3, Line 16. Algorithm 5.4 implements the procedure triggered by the arrival of an update at the *remote reasoner*. Rule R is reevaluated to obtain a new set of tuples S (Line 2). The new result S is compared with the previous one stored $LastResult$ and if they are different from each other (Lines 3 and 4), this result is stored as $LastResult$ (Line 5) and sent to the *local reasoner* as a notification (Line 6).

Algorithm 5.5 implements the procedure triggered by the arrival of a notification from the *remote reasoner* at the *local reasoner*. In this case, the *local reasoner* compares the number of the update n, provided with the notification, with the last $UpdateNumber$ associated with that rule R (Line 1). If they are equal, the result S is sent to the client application (Line 2). Otherwise, the result is ignored.

Algorithm 5.5: ON RECEIVING NOTIFICATION FROM PEER

---

input: An notification message containing a set of values S and a version number n.

1 **if** $N = UpdateNumber$ **then**
2   Notifies the client C with result S
3 **end**

Fig. 5.3 Synchronous interaction in the cooperative
reasoning

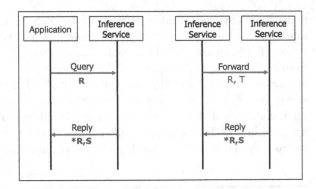

Finally, Algorithm 5.6 implements the procedure triggered by the arrival of a
message from the client asking to remove the subscription associated with a rule R.
If R has a *remote part* R_R, the *local reasoner* has to send a removal message to
the *remote reasoner* asking for the removal of the subscription associated with R_R
(Line 2). In any case, R is removed by the *local reasoner* (Line 4).

Algorithm 5.6: ON RECEIVING REMOVAL ASK

---

input: An message asking the removal of rule R.

1 **if** $R_R \neq \emptyset$ **then**
2   Removes R_R from the remote reasoner
3 **end**
4 Removes R from list L

5.3 Protocol

The reasoning process discussed in Sect. 5.1 is implemented as a service that
receives messages from client applications—*synchronous queries* or *subscriptions*—
containing rules that describe situations that are relevant for these applications. The
reasoning process is performed by services, the *cooperative reasoners*, that exchange
messages to execute the distributed algorithm described in Sect. 5.2. Nevertheless,
the overall *cooperative reasoning process* is only completely specified after we define
a communication protocol, describing all the messages exchanged by these services.
As we assume that the communication channel is reliable, i.e., there is no loss of
messages, confirmations messages were not included in our protocol.

Figure 5.3 shows the protocol executed for performing the synchronous interaction
of our cooperative reasoning process, as described in Sect. 5.1.1. The synchronous
interaction starts when a Query message is sent from the client to the *local reasoner*, with rule R as parameter, triggering the procedure described in Algorithm 5.1

Table 5.1 The protocol executed for performing the synchronous interaction of our cooperative reasoning process

Operation	Description
Query(R)	A client application sends a message to the local reasoner with a rule R, which describes the situation to be verified.
Forward(R_R, V, T)	The local reasoner sends to the remote reasoner this message containing R_R, the remote part of the original rule, the list of variables V that were evaluated locally and the set T of tuples with values for each variable.
Reply (S)	The local reasoner sends a message to a client—or the remote reasoner sends a message to the local reasoner—as a response to a synchronous query, containing a set of matches S that satisfy the originally proposed rule R.

(Step S1). A Forward message is sent from the *local reasoner* to the *remote reasoner*, carrying the *remote part* of the rule R_R, if it exists, together with the set of variables V and the set of tuples T determined in the pre-evaluation of R (Steps S2, S3 e S4). The rule forwarded by the *local reasoner* is received by the *remote reasoner* as a query with some extra parameters, and regarded as a *local rule*. It is evaluated by the *remote reasoner*, and the set of tuples S, found as result of the evaluation, is sent back to the *local reasoner* in a Reply message (Step S5). The *local reasoner* waits for this response (Step S6), and after receiving it, sends a Reply message to the client application containing this answer (Step S7). When the original rule is local, the only message sent is the Reply message containing the set of tuples S from the *local reasoner* to the client application (Step S7). Table 5.1 summarizes the synchronous protocol.

The messages exchanged in an asynchronous interaction are shown in Fig. 5.4. This interaction starts when a Subscribe message is sent from the client to the *local reasoner*, with the rule R as parameter (Step S1). This message triggers the procedure described in Algorithm 5.2. A Forward message is sent from the *local reasoner* to the *remote reasoner* if R has a *remote part* R_R (Steps S2, S3 e S4), with R_R together with the set of variables V and the set of tuples T, determined in the pre-evaluation, as parameters.

An Update message is sent from the *local reasoner* to the *remote reasoner*, with a reference to rule R_R, the new set of tuples T and $UpdateNumber$ as parameters, whenever a change in context data in the *local reasoner* causes T to change (Steps S8, S9, S10 e S12). This message triggers the procedure described in Algorithm 5.4.

A Notify message is sent from the *local reasoner* to the client application, with the result S as parameter, after the first evaluation of R (if S is not empty, Step S5) and whenever a change in context data in the *local reasoner* causes S to change (Steps S8,

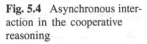

Fig. 5.4 Asynchronous interaction in the cooperative
reasoning

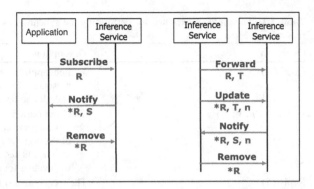

S9, S10 e S11). A `Notify` message may also be sent from the *remote reasoner* to
the *local reasoner* whenever a change in context data in the *remote reasoner* causes
the result S associated with a *forwarded rule* R_R to change, with the result S and
the *LastUpdateNumber* as parameters (Steps S8, S9, S10 e S11). This message
triggers the procedure described in Algorithm 5.5. In this case, another `Notify`
message is sent from the *local reasoner* to the client application, with the result S as
parameter, if the *LastUpdateNumber* received by the *local reasoner* has the same
value of the local variable *UpdateNumber* (Step S11).

The `Remove` message, sent from the client to *local reasoner*, triggers the procedure described in Algorithm 5.6. If the rule to be removed has a *remote part*, a
`Remove` message is sent from the *local reasoner* to the *remote reasoner*, with a reference for rule R as parameter (Step S13). Table 5.2 summarizes the asynchronous
approach.

5.4 Discussion

In this chapter, we proposed a strategy to execute *cooperative reasoning* and described
the distributed algorithm and communication protocol to perform the complete
process, according with the functional attributes of the design stratagies that we
enumeratad in Sect. 4.3.

A fundamental part of our proposal for the split inference of facts is the partitioning
of a rule in its local part, that is evaluated by the *local reasoner*, and its remote part,
which is forwarded to the *remote reasoner*. When there are context variables that are
common to the local and the remote part of the rules, however, the *remote reasoner*—
to be able to evaluate the remote part of the rule—needs to know which are the
possible values that the common variables may assume. As explained in Sect. 5.1,
this is achieved by the Pre-evaluation/Forwarding and Reevaluation/Update steps
of the reasoning strategy. These steps are associated with the *Update* and *Forward*
messages, whose content comprises the tuples corresponding to the possible values

Table 5.2 The protocol executed for performing the asynchronous interaction of our cooperative reasoning process

Operation	Description
Subscribe(R)	A client application sends a message to the local reasoner with a rule R describing a situation of interest.
Forward(R_R, V, T)	The local reasoner sends this message to the remote reasoner containing R_R, the remote part of the original rule, the list of variables V that were evaluated locally and the set T of tuples with values for each variable.
Update($*R_R$, T, n)	The local reasoner sends this message to the remote reasoner containing a reference to the rule R_R, previously forwarded, updated information to the corresponding set of tuples T and an update number n that identifies the update version.
Notify($*R$, S [, n])	The local reasoner sends this message to the client application—or the remote reasoner sends the message to the local reasoner—containing a reference to a rule R previously provided to the reasoner and a set of matches S that satisfy the rule R. If the notification is sent by the remote reasoner to the local reasoner, it contains also the number of the last update received by the sender n.
Remove($*R$)	A client application sends the message to the local reasoner—or the local reasoner sends the message to the remote reasoner—containing a reference to a rule R previously submitted, whose corresponding subscription must be removed.

that the set of variables may assume. In the reasoning process, these tuples represent a partial result for the *local reasoner* and a starting point for the *remote reasoner*. As the *local reasoner* forwards no complete RDF tuple for the *remote reasoner*, only tuples of individuals representing context variable values, no knowledge sharing happens between those reasoners. Particularly, when there is no variable in common between the local and remote parts of the rule, the variable values have to be solely determined in each side.

Providing asynchronous communication (publish/subscribe) is a particularly important attribute identified for this inference service. To achieve this goal, a *local reasoner* has to constantly update the information forwarded to the *remote reasoner*, in the *cooperative interaction*. For that reason, if there are frequent context changes at the *local reasoner*, not only the reasoning operation may never converge, bu also the great number of messages exchanged between the reasoners may cause a great communication overhead. This means that the proposed strategy is not adequate for reasoning with highly variable context data.

In our proposal of a *cooperative reasoning* protocol, however, we did not accounted for aspects related with an important non-functional attribute, the robustness and resilience of the service. In our system model we assumed that the communication was reliable, i.e., there would be no loss of messages. As such, we did not include confirmation messages in our protocol, and hence, the loss of a message can cause an inference operation to be discontinued, with no warning being sent to the clients.

In the next chapter, we present a case study to show how—step-by-step—this strategy works, both for synchronous communication (queries) and asynchronous communication (publish/subscribe).

Chapter 6
Case Study

Abstract This chapter shows how the strategy proposed in the previous chapter
works for a realistic scenario, such as the one described in Sect. 2.1. We present two
different examples, a client query (synchronous interaction) and a client
subscription (asynchronous interaction). For both cases we assume that the context
data distribution corresponds to what was shown in Fig. 4.1.

Keywords Ambient intelligence, Ubiquitous computing, Context-awareness, Rule-
based reasoning, Decentralized reasoning, Cooperative reasoning

6.1 Synchronous Interaction

At first, let us consider that Rule 6.1 was submitted (Step S1) by a client application
as a *synchronous query*. This rule says that "if Silva is located in a room, where some
activity is taking place, and if this activity has already started, then Silva is busy."
The inference of this rule consists in finding values for the pair of variables "?s" and
"?r", i.e., a set of tuples (s_i, r_i), that make true the atoms of the antecedent of the
rule.

Rule 6.1:

$$isLocatedIn("Silva", ?r) \land takesPlace(?s, ?r) \land hasStarted(?s) \longrightarrow$$
$$isBusyInActivity("Silva", ?s)$$

Looking at Fig. 4.1, we can notice that the context information necessary for
detecting the situation described by this rule comprises data related to the user's
preferences and data collected from the device (Silva's location) and information
about the event (room where a session "takes place" and the fact that it "has started").
In our scenario, while the first piece of information is originated and managed at the
mobile device, the latter two pieces are managed by the ambient infrastructure.

J. Viterbo and M. Endler, *Decentralized Reasoning in Ambient Intelligence*,
SpringerBriefs in Computer Science, DOI: 10.1007/978-1-4471-4168-6_6,
© The Author(s) 2012

In the next step, the rule has to be partitioned (Step S2) to identify which part of R may be dealt at each side of the system. This rule would be split in the *local part* R_L, described as Rule 6.2, and the *remote part* R_R, described as Rule 6.3. Variable "?r" is an example of a variable that has to be pre-evaluated by the *local reasoner*, because the information about the predicate "isLocated" is available only at the *user side*, but the variable is present both in R_L and R_R. In this case, the set of variables that are common in both parts of the rule consists in the unitary set $V = \{?r\}$.

Rule 6.2:

$$isLocatedIn(\text{"}Silva\text{"},?r)$$

Rule 6.3:

$$takesPlace(?s,?r) \wedge hasStarted(?s)$$

After the pre-evaluation of the variable "?r" by the *local reasoner* (Step S3), we find the set of values for "?r" as the unitary set $T = \{\text{"}Room\_B\text{"}\}$. In the next step, R_R, T and V, are forwarded to the *remote reasoner* (Step S4). The evaluation of the *forwarded rule* by the *remote reasoner* (Step S5) under the restrictions imposed by the set of values T for the variables in V is equivalent, in this case, to the evaluation of the Rule 6.4 in which "?r" assumes the value "Room_B".

Rule 6.4:

$$takesPlace(?s,\text{"}Room\_B\text{"}) \wedge hasStarted(?s) \longrightarrow isBusyInActivity(\text{"}Silva\text{"},?s)$$

The result of the evaluation of this rule, based on the data available on the *ambient side* (Fig. 4.1), would be the unitary set $S = \{\text{"}Session\_2\text{"}\}$. This result would be sent by the *remote reasoner* (Step S7) to the *local reasoner* (Step S6), that would send the result to the client application (Step S6), meaning that at that time, "Silva is busy participating in Session 2."

6.2 Asynchronous Interaction

Let us now consider that Rule 6.5 has been submitted by an application (Step S1) as a *subscription*. This rule says that "if an activity that Silva wants to attend is about to start and he is located in a room different from the one where the activity takes place, then he should go to that room." In this case, the inference of this rule consists in finding values for the tuples of variables "?s", "?x" and "?y" that make true the antecedent of the rule.

Rule 6.5:

$$wantsToAttend(\text{"}Silva\text{"},?s) \wedge isLocatedIn(\text{"}Silva\text{"},?y) \wedge takesPlace(?s,?x) \wedge$$
$$differentFrom(?y,?x) \wedge isAboutToStart(?s) \longrightarrow shouldGoTo(\text{"}Silva\text{"},?x)$$

As in the first example, the atoms in this rule comprise data available both at the *user side*, such as information about the user's preferences (sessions that Silva "wants to attend" and his location), and the *ambient side*, such as information about the activities (room where a session "takes place" and the fact that it "is about to start").

In the next step (Step S2), R would be partitioned in the *local part* R_L and the *remote part* R_R, as described by Rules 4.9 and 4.10, respectively.

Rule 6.6:

$$wantsToAttend(\text{``Silva''}, ?s) \wedge isLocatedIn(\text{``Silva''}, ?y)$$

Rule 6.7:

$$takesPlace(?s, ?x) \wedge differentFrom(?y, ?x) \wedge isAboutToStart(?s)$$

We can identify that the set of variables that are common in R_L and R_R is $V = \{?y, ?s\}$. In the pre-evaluation of R_L (Step S3) we determine that there is a single value for the variable "$?y$", which is "Room_B", while there are four different values that satisfy the variable "$?s$", which are "Session_1", "Session_2", "Session_3" and "Session_4". In practice, we have a set of four tuples that represent values for the variables in V that make R_L true, such that $T = \{(\text{``Room\_B''}, \text{``Session\_1''}), (\text{``Room\_B''}, \text{``Session\_2''}), (\text{``Room\_B''}, \text{``Session\_3''}), (\text{``Room\_B''}, \text{``Session\_4''})\}$.

The next step is then the forwarding of R_R (Step S4) to the *remote reasoner* with the correspondent sets V and T. In this case, the *remote reasoner* receives the *forwarded rule* as a *subscription*, and the execution of a first evaluation of the rule (Step S5) produces a void result, i.e., there is no such a tuple of values for "$?y$", "$?s$" and "$?x$" that make Rule 6.7 true. The *remote reasoner* adds the *forwarded rule* to a list of subscriptions and starts to monitor the context variables present in that rule (Step S8). Therefore, if there is any change in facts involving the predicates *takesPlace* or *isAboutToStart*, the rule is reevaluated (Step S9). For instance, if the fact *isAboutToStart("Session_4")* is added to the ABox on the *ambient side*, the rule R_R is reevaluated and the result would be the unitary set $S = \{\text{``Room\_A''}\}$. This result would be notified to the *local reasoner* (Step S11), which would send it to the client application, meaning that "Silva should go to Room A".

At the *local reasoner*, the *local part* of the rule R_L is put in a list of subscriptions and the respective context variables are monitored by *local reasoner* (Step S8). If any change involving the predicates *wantsToAttend* or *isLocatedIn* occurs, the rule is reevaluated (Step S9). For instance, if there is a change so that the fact *wantsToAttend("Silva", "Session_2")* is removed from the ABox on the *user side*, R_L would be reevaluated and the result would be a new set T, different from the previously found (Step S10). The *local reasoner* would update this information sending the new set T with an update number to the *remote reasoner* (Step S12). As we discussed in Sect. 5.1.3, whenever a context change happens and T changes, there will be a new update associated with an exclusive update number. When a result is received from the *remote reasoner*, it carries the number that was provided with the last update, so as to enable the *local reasoner* to check if the result is valid and may be sent to the client application.

6.3 Discussion

In this chapter we exemplified how the cooperative reasoning strategy works for client queries and client subscriptions. We discussed each step of the proposed strategy, explaining the obtained results. Through this example, we could demonstrate the adequability of this approach for a common AmI scenario, as discussed in Sect. 5.1.3.

Chapter 7
Implementation

Abstract In this chapter we describe the Decentralized Reasoning Service (DRS), a prototype service implementation that performs the cooperative reasoning process presented before. We present also the Context Model Service (CMS), another prototype service that had to be to implemented to support the DRS providing access to up-to-date context information. Finally, to show how the use of the DRS simplifies the design of ubiquitous applications, we discuss the use of context and inference services in the implementation of a prototype application.

Keywords Ambient Intelligence · Ubiquitous computing · Context-awareness · Rule-based reasoning · Decentralized reasoning · Cooperative reasoning · Publish-subscribe

7.1 Architecture Overview

We implemented the Decentralized Reasoning Service (DRS) as a prototype service that implements our approach proposed for decentralized reasoning, performing the *cooperative reasoning process* described in Chap. 5. This rule-based inference service was designed to be executed on top of a middleware architecture aiming to provide a complete infrastructure to create context-aware applications integrating mobile devices and multiple context providers in AmI environments.

To be able to test and evaluate the DRS, it was absolutely necessary to have the functionalities provided by a service responsible for managing context information, i.e., collecting, storing and providing access to context data. As such, we implemented also the Context Model Service (CMS), a prototype service responsible for collecting context data from context providers available in a specific domain, keeping an updated representation of the assembled data according to a valid context model (an ontology), and providing access to up-to-date context information.

J. Viterbo and M. Endler, *Decentralized Reasoning in Ambient Intelligence*, 67
SpringerBriefs in Computer Science, DOI: 10.1007/978-1-4471-4168-6_7,
© The Author(s) 2012

CMS is described in more detail in Sect. 7.3, while the characteristics of the DRS implementation are discussed in Sect. 7.4. As both CMS and DRS rely on KAON2 [11]—an OWL and reasoning API—to access ontology data and perform reasoning operations, this API is further described in the next section. In our scenario we assumed that all entities share the same context model (ontology) and every DRS and CMS server has a well-known address (IP and port).

7.2 Ontology Management and Reasoning

Various reasoning engines have been developed for reasoning and querying OWL-DL ontologies, implementing different reasoning algorithms and optimization techniques, hence differing in a number of ways [9]. Systems such as RACER [7], Pellet [12] and KAON2 [11] provide automated reasoning support for checking concepts for satisfiability and subsumption in a *TBox*, and also for answering rule-based queries, retrieving the individuals in an *ABox* that satisfy a given rule [5].

KAON2 has been compared with RACER and Pellet [1, 4, 11] and it was found that it provides better performance for ontologies with rather simple *TBoxes*, but large *ABoxes* [10], i.e., ontologies with a large number of individuals and facts and a small number of classes and properties. In contrast, for ontologies with large and complex TBoxes, the other reasoners provide superior performance. Furthermore, among these three reasoners, KAON2 has as distinguished features its simplicity and compactness, as it includes an API for managing OWL ontologies, while Pellet and RACER require the use of specific tools as the OWL API [8]. As ontologies for ubiquitous computing scenarios tend to have large *ABoxes* while *TBoxes* are not so large nor complex [15], and given the simplicity of KAON2, we assumed it was more appropriate for ubiquitous scenarios such as the one described in Sect. 2.1. Hence, we selected KAON2 to implement ontology management and reasoning for our CMS and DRS.

KAON2 is an OWL-DL reasoner implemented in Java 1.5 and free for non-commercial use. Differently from RACER and Pellet, KAON2 does not implement the tableau calculus, but rather transforms OWL-DL ontologies into disjunctive datalog, and applies established algorithms for dealing with this formalism, enabling a faster processing of large *ABoxes*. The system can decide concept satisfiability, compute the subsumption hierarchy, and answer conjunctive queries in which all variables are distinguished [6].

It can be used as a stand-alone server or as a dynamic library, providing an Ontology API and a Reasoning API. The Ontology API—which is used by CMS—provides ontology manipulation services, such as adding and retrieving ontology axioms. The API fully supports OWL and the Semantic Web Rule Language (SWRL) at the syntactic level. It allows ontologies to be saved in files using either OWL-RDF or OWL-XML syntax. The Reasoning API—which is used by DRS—allows to invoke various reasoning functionalities and to retrieve their results. We used the latest stable release of KAON2, published on 29th of June 2008.

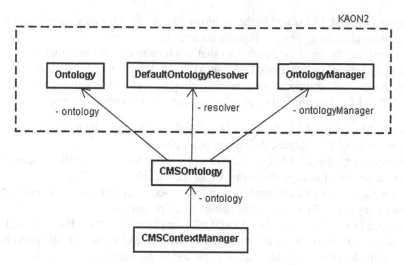

Fig. 7.1 Class diagram showing the implementation of the CMS server

7.3 Context Model Service (CMS)

In our middleware architecture for ubiquitous environments, the Context Model Service (CMS) was implemented as the basic service responsible for collecting all context data from the context providers available in a given domain and keeping an updated representation of the assembled data coherent with the adopted context model. These context provider may be any sensor, service or applications that sends data to CMS, which are interpreted and stores as facts according with the ontology. Besides that, the CMS provides access to up-to-date context data for DRS and applications that need plain context information, i.e., that does not involve reasoning.

CMS was implemented in Java (version 1.6.0) as a multi-threaded server that supports synchronous communication using both TCP and UDP transport layer protocols. Since it does not implement context monitoring (which is implemented only by the DRS), CMS does not provide asynchronous (event-based) communication. CMS uses KAON2 API—discussed in the last section—to manipulate the context ontology database and MoCA communication APIs [14] to implement synchronous communication. Figure 7.1 shows a simplified class diagram of the CMS service implementation, in which the main dependencies on KAON2 classes are represented. The main class of the service is the *CMSContextManager*, which implements the communication and the server loop to receive message from client applications. This class relies on class *CMSOntology* to access and manage a specific ontology. Class *CMSOntology* uses KAON2 classes *Ontology*, *DefaultOntologyManager* and *OntologyManager* to manage an OWL ontology file.

In practice, CMS is a server that when started loads up a configuration file ("cms.properties") that defines the IP address, port and protocol (UDP or TCP) for running the server, and an ontology file to be loaded. The server will load the context model and data stored in the ontology file and wait for messages from client applications consulting or updating this context data.

To facilitate the work of developers that implement context provider or context consumer applications we created a client API for CMS. The *CMSClient* API implements the methods enumerated below, providing a greater abstraction level than the KAON2 API for describing the providing or consulting context information.

- `ArrayList getAllClasses()`—Used by a client application to retrieve, as an array list of RDF tuples, the names of all classes.
- `ArrayList getAllIndividuals()`—Used by a client application to retrieve, as an array list of strings, the names of all individuals.
- `ArrayList getAllProperties()`—Used by a client application to retrieve, as an array list of RDF tuples, the names of all properties.
- `ArrayList getIndividualsOfClass(String C)`—Used by a client application to retrieve, as an array list of strings, the names of all individuals belonging to a class C, whose name is passed as parameter.
- `ArrayList getIndividualsOfProperty(String P)`—Used by a client application to retrieve, as an array list of strings, the names of all individuals having a property P, whose name is passed as parameter.
- `ArrayList getPropertiesOfIndividuals(String I)`—Used by a client application to retrieve, as an array list of RDF tuples, all the properties of an individuals I, whose name is passed as parameter.
- `void register(String pred, String subj, String obj)`— Used by a context provider to register at CMS and provide some context data regularly, in the form of a RDF tuple.
- `void include(ArrayList L)`—Used by a context provider to send a list of context data, as an array list of RDF tuples, to be included in CMS database.
- `void remove(ArrayList L)`—Used by a context provider to send a list of context data, as an array list of RDF tuples, to be removed from CMS database.
- `void update(String pred, String subj, String obj)`—Used by a context provider to update a specific context data piece, in the form of an RDF tuple.

7.4 The Decentralized Reasoning Service (DRS)

The Decentralized Reasoning Service (DRS) was implemented to provide reasoning services for application clients, not only in synchronous mode (queries) but also in asynchronous mode (publish/subscribe interactions), according to the design strategies enumerated in Sect. 4.3. It relies on the CMS server to access context data and monitor context data changes, and is capable of reasoning about rules provided by client applications.

DRS was implemented in Java (version 1.6.0) as a multi-threaded server supporting both synchronous and asynchronous (event-based) communication, using either

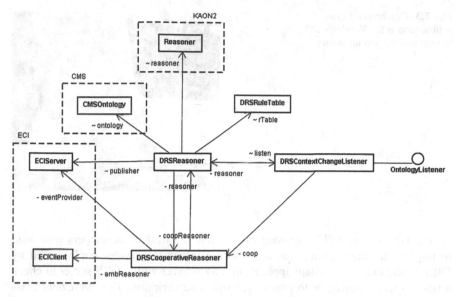

Fig. 7.2 Class diagram showing the implementation of the DRS server

TCP or UDP protocols. DRS uses *CMS* API to access the corresponding ontology and KAON2 API to implement the reasoning operations over the context ontology database. Besides that, it uses MoCA's communication API [14] to implement event-based communication. Figure 7.2 depicts the class dependency showing a simplified class diagram of the DRS service implementation. The main class of the service is the *DRSReasoner*, which implements the communication and the server loop to cope with messages received from client applications. This class relies on class *CMSOntology* to access data from specific ontology, class *ECIServer* to provide an event-based interface to client applications and the *peer reasoner*, class *ECIClient* to subscribe at the *peer reasoner* and class *Reasoner* to perform reasoning operations. While synchronous queries are immediately managed by DRS, subscriptions require the use of specific data structures for keeping the information associated with each active subscription. Class *DRSRuleTable* is used to keep all information related with a received subscription, such as the associated rule and the latest result found. Class *DRSCooperativeReasoner* is responsible for managing operations related with rules that are not local, such as *pre-evaluation*, *forwarding* and *update* (discussed in Sect. 5.1.2). Finally, class *DRSContextChangeListener* is used to trigger the *reevaluation* of any rule associated with context data that was subject of changes. It is implemented extending the *OntologyChangeListener* interface, part of the KAON2 API.

When executing the DRS server, after start up it loads up a configuration file ("drs.properties"), which defines the IP address and protocol (UDP or TCP) for running the server, assigning different ports for receiving synchronous queries and for receiving subscriptions.

Fig. 7.3 Conference Companion icon at the Windows
toolbar and the pop-up menu

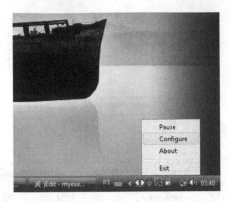

The DRS Client API is provided to facilitate the work of developers who want
to implement client applications that use the inference services implemented by
DRS. Using this API, a client application may interact with a DRS server to check
a rule (synchronously), or to post or remove a subscription. The *DRSClient* class
implements the methods describe ahead.

- `ArrayList checkRule(DRSRule R)`—Checks the result of a query for the
  rule *R*, passed as parameter, in a synchronous interaction. The result is an array
  list of RDF triples corresponding to binary or unary facts correlating individuals
  that satisfy the rule.
- `subscribe(DRSRule R, EventListener e)`—Subscribes at DRS, with
  a request to be notified about the result of the rule *R* passed as parameter, together
  with a listener that represents a callback routine.
- `unsubscribe(DRSRule R, EventListener e)`—Removes the subscription related to rule *R*.

In the next section we exemplify how these methods can be used to build a
prototype application.

7.5 Prototype Application

To show how DRS may be used to support the implementation and execution of
a ubiquitous application, we present the main steps of the design of a prototype
application. We chose to implement a simplified version of the application proposed
in our scenario, the Conference Companion (ConfComp), which was discussed in
Sect. 2.1. This application aims to help the user with his agenda during a conference
event and to stimulate the collaboration and social interaction with other researchers
attending the event, by helping the user to locate people with similar interests.

ConfComp is a simple application that—after started and configured—runs in
background, occasionally providing notifications for the user. Figure 7.3 shows the

Fig. 7.4 Block diagram representing the interaction among the applications and the middleware services DRS and CMS on the *user side* and the *ambient side*

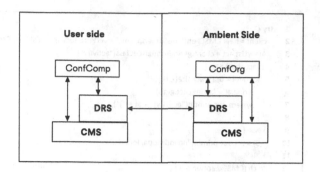

icon of the application at the Windows toolbar and the menu that pops up when the user clicks the right button of the mouse with it over this icon. In the menu we see the options "Exit", "About", "Configure" and "Pause". If the "Exit" option is selected, the program is terminated. The selection of the "About" option causes a window showing information about the program to pop up. The option "Configure" shows a window that allows the user to select the sessions of the conference in which he is interested. After that, each time a session in which the user is interested is about to start, the application shows a pop up window warning the user about the event.

In order to demonstrate how the use of the DRS service and APIs simplify the design of ubiquitous applications, we will discuss some aspects of the implementation of the prototype related to the use of context and the inference services. As such, the implementation of the user interface will not be in the scope of this text. Figure 7.4 shows a block diagram of the prototype system, where applications interact directly with the middleware services in the same side. In our example, ConfComp sends context queries (about activities) and updates (about the user's preferences) to the local CMS and subscribes at the local DRS for having a rule inferred. The local services are in charge of interacting with the remote services.

The first step performed by this application is to query the CMS running at the *user side* to get a list of activities, i.e., scheduled conference sessions. Figure 7.5 shows the piece of Java code that corresponds to this operation. At Line 2 an object *client*, instance of the class *CMSClient*, is created, having as parameters the IP and port of the CMS server and the application, and the communication protocol. At Line 3 we can see a call to the method *getIndividualOfClass* in which the parameter "activity" is used to recover all individuals of such class (e.g., *Session_1*, *Session_2*, etc.). At Line 12 we see the statement for catching the *CMSException*, that may be thrown if the communication with CMS fails.

When the user wants to set the list of sessions that he wishes to attend, he has to select the "Configure" option of the pop-up menu and the window depicted in Figure 7.6 will be shown. In this window, the user must select the names of the sessions that are of his interest and press the "Ok" button. The application will send this information to local CMS. Figure 7.7 shows the Java code that performs this operation. From Lines 1 to 6 an array list is created containing the new facts to be added to the ontology in the local CMS. These facts are of class *CMSAtom*, that

```
 1    try {
 2        client = new CMSClient(cmsServerIp, cmsServerPort, localIp, localPort, CMSConstants.UDP);
 3        ArrayList act = client.getIndividualsOfClass("activity");
 4        if (act.size() > 0) {
 5            for (int i = 0; i < act.size(); i++) {
 6                String at = (String) act.get(i);
 7                System.out.println("activity(" + at + ")");
 8            }
 9        } else {
10            System.out.println("no individual found...");
11        }
12    } catch (CMSException ex) {
13        Logger.getLogger(ConfComp.class.getName()).log(Level.SEVERE, null, ex);
14    }
```

Fig. 7.5 Code snippet showing the query to get all "activities" from CMS

Fig. 7.6 GUI for the user to
set the list of sessions he wants
to attend

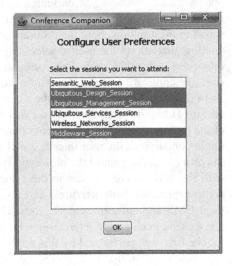

describe ontology facts as RDF tuples, with a predicate, a subject and an object.
At Line 8 we can see the invocation of the method *include* in the *CMSClient* object,
which had been previously instantiated (Fig. 7.5, Line 2). The parameter for this
method is the variable *pref*, an array list of *CMSAtom* objects representing facts
$wantsToAttend(Silva, Session_i)$, where $Session_i$ is each session indicated by
the user. *CMSException* may be thrown if the communication with CMS fails.

After the user has set the list of sessions, the next step for the application is to
subscribe at the DRS running at the *user side*, providing a rule to be monitored by
the reasoner. For our application, Rule 7.1 below describes the situation in which
"a session that the user wants to attend is about to start and he is outside the respective
room".

```
1    ArrayList pref = new ArrayList();
2    try {
3        CMSAtom a;
4        for (int i = 0; i < o.length; i++) {
5            a = new CMSAtom("wantsToAttend", "Silva", (String) o[i]);
6            pref.add(a);
7        }
8        client.include(pref);
9    } catch (CMSException ex) {
10       Logger.getLogger(ConfComp.class.getName()).log(Level.SEVERE, null, ex);
11   }
```

Fig. 7.7 Code snippet showing an update of data in the CMS

```
1    DRSRule R = new DRSRule(2);
2    R.addAtomtoAntecedent(new DRSAtom("wantsToAttend", new DRSTerm(1, "Silva"), new DRSTerm(0, "S")));
3    R.addAtomtoAntecedent(new DRSAtom("takesPlace", new DRSTerm(0, "S"), new DRSTerm(0, "R")));
4    R.addAtomtoAntecedent(new DRSAtom("isAboutToStart", new DRSTerm(0, "S")));
5    R.addAtomtoAntecedent(new DRSAtom("isLocatedIn", new DRSTerm(1, "Silva"), new DRSTerm(0, "T")));
6    R.addAtomtoAntecedent(new DRSAtom("differentFrom", new DRSTerm(0, "S"), new DRSTerm(0, "T")));
7    R.setConsequent(new DRSAtom("isStartingIn", new DRSTerm(0, "S"), new DRSTerm(0, "R")));
```

Fig. 7.8 Code snippet showing the description of a rule

Rule 7.1:

$$isInterestedIn(``Silva",?s) \wedge takesPlace(?s,?r) \wedge isAboutToStart(?s) \wedge$$
$$isLocatedIn(``Silva",?t) \wedge isDifferentFrom(?t,?r) \Rightarrow isStartingIn(?s,?r)$$

Figure 7.8 shows the Java code used to create a rule object corresponding to Rule 7.1. At Line 1 a new *DRSRule* object is instantiated. From Lines 2 to 6 new atoms are added to the antecedent of the rule, each corresponding to one of the five atoms presented in Rule 7.1. At Line 7 the consequent of the rule is defined.

Figure 7.9 shows the Java code used to subscribe at a DRS, having the rule *R* to be monitored as a parameter. At Line 2 an object *reasoner*, instance of the class *DRSClient*, is created, having as parameters the IP and port of the DRS server and the application, and the communication protocol to be used. At Line 3 we can see an invocation of the method *subscribe* of the object *reasoner*, in which the parameters are the *DRSRule* object *R* and a *EventListener* object *MyEventListener*. As a result, this rule is sent to DRS as a subscription and any notification will trigger the event listener *listener*, which will cope with the received result. At Line 4 a *DRSException* exception is caught if the communication with DRS fails.

As a mean of notifying the user, the application shall pop up a window with a message warning the user about the session that is going to start, so that he can go to the respective room where the activity will take place. Figure 7.10 shows the Java code that describes the class *MyEventListener*, which implements the interface

```
1    try {
2        reasoner = new DRSClient(drsServerIp, drsServerPort, localIp, localPort, DRSConstants.UDP);
3        reasoner.subscribe(R, MyEventListener);
4    } catch (DRSException ex) {
5        Logger.getLogger(ConfComp.class.getName()).log(Level.SEVERE, null, ex);
6    }
```

Fig. 7.9 Code snippet showing the subscription

```
1    public class MyEventListener implements EventListener {
2        public void onReceiveData(Event receivedEvent) {
3            DRSReply q = (DRSReply) receivedEvent.getData();
4            ArrayList matches = q.getMatches();
5            for (int i = 0; i < matches.size(); i++) {
6                DRSAtom atom = (DRSAtom) matches.get(i);
7                String m = "User should go to "+atom.getObj().getTerm()+" now to attend "+atom.getSubj().getTerm()";
8                JOptionPane.showMessageDialog(null,m,"Conference Companion",JOptionPane.WARNING_MESSAGE);
9            }
10       }
11   }
```

Fig. 7.10 Code snippet showing the implementation of the event listener

Fig. 7.11 Window that pops
up to warn the user that a
session he wants to attend is
going to begin

EventListener defining the action to be taken when an notification arrives from the
DRS.

The notification triggers the *listener*, having an *Event* object as parameter.
At Line 3 of Fig. 7.10, the method *getData* is used to get the content brought in
the *Event* object. This content is a *DRSReply* object, which contains an arraylist of
atoms, each corresponding to a fact in the ontology database that satisfies Rule 7.1, i.e.
assertions in the form *isStartingIn(?s, ?r)*. At Line 6, an atom from the list is selected
and, at Line 7, the subject and object of each atom representing a binary property
assertion—e.g. *isStartingIn(MiddlewareSession, Room_A*—are used to compose the
message to be displayed to the user. At Line 8, we show the window described in
Fig. 7.11. This warning message will pop up each time a new notification about an
activity arrives at the client application.

7.6 Discussion

In this chapter, we described our prototype implementations of the Context Model Service (CMS) and the Decentralized Reasoning Service (DRS). The CMS is the service responsible for collecting context data from context providers available in a specific domain, keeping an updated representation of the assembled data according to a valid context model (an ontology), and providing access to up-to-date context information. The DRS is the service that implements the *cooperative reasoning process*, providing reasoning services for application clients in synchronous mode (queries) and in asynchronous mode (publish/subscribe interactions).

To be used in real world AmI scenarios, dealing with the dynamic and heterogeneous characteristics of such environments, these services should be executed on top of a more complex middleware architecture, capable of providing complementary functionalities such as service discovery [13], or support to semantic interoperability [2, 3]. In the absence of such services, we greatly simplified the model of our system, assuming that all entities shared a same context model and the DRS and CMS servers had well-known communication addresses.

CMS and DRS were implemented using the KAON2 reasoning API to access ontology data and perform reasoning operations. Although our implementation of the services has a small memory footprint—20.2 KB—, as KAON2 was available only for J2SE environment, it was not possible to implement our services targeting mobile devices, which execute only J2ME based applications. We believe, however, that in the future these implementations may be ported to the mobile environment. In this case, the interfaces provided by our CMS and DRS APIs will not be modified, and the implementation applications for mobile devices will follow the same model discussed in Sect. 7.5.

A programmer who wants to design ubiquitous applications will have his work facilitated by the CMS and DRS services and APIs, as he will be able to use rules as an abstraction to describe the situations of interest for his application. On the other hand, in a system where the context model is not as simple as the one presented in our scenario, formulating the necessary rules may be a hard task for the programmer, demanding a great knowledge about the context model of the target system and some acquaintance with description logics. In this case, tools or interfaces that help the programmer to formulate and validate these rules would be an important complement to be developed and added to DRS.

References

1. Bock, J., Haase, P., Ji, Q., Volz, R.: Benchmarking OWL reasoners. In: Proceedings of the Workshop on Advancing Reasoning on the Web: Scalability and Commonsense (ARea08), CEUR Workshop Proceedings (2008)
2. Breitman, K., Brauner, D., Casanova, M., Milidiú, R., Perazolo, A.: Instance-based ontology mapping. In: Proceedings of the Fourth IEEE International Workshop on Engineering of

Autonomic and Autonomous Systems EASe 2007, pp. 117–126. IEEE Computer Society Press (2007)

3. Felicíssimo, C., Breitman, K.: Taxonomic ontology alignment—an implementation. In: Proceedings of Workshop em Engenharia de Requisitos (WER 2004), pp. 152–163 (2004)

4. Gardiner, T., Tsarkov, D., Horrocks, I.: Framework for an automated comparison of description logic reasoners. In: Proceedings of 5th International Semantic Web Conference (ISWC 2006). Springer Verlag (2006)

5. Glimm, B., Horrocks, I., Lutz, C., Sattler, U.: Conjunctive query answering for the description logic SHIQ. In: Proceedings of the 20th International Joint Conference on Artificial Intelligence (IJCAI 2007) (2007)

6. Glimm, B., Horrocks, I., Sattler, U.: Conjunctive query answering for description logics with transitive roles. In: Proceedings of the 2006 Description Logic Workshop (DL 2006), CEUR Workshop Proceedings (2006)

7. Haarslev, V., Möller, R.: RACER System Description. In: Proceedings of the International Joint Conference on Automated Reasoning (IJCAR'01), Lecture Notes in Computer Science, vol. 2083 (2001)

8. Horridge, M., Bechhofer, S., Noppens, O.: Igniting the OWL 1.1 touch paper: the OWL API. In: CEUR Proceedings of 3rd OWL Experiences and Directions Workshop (OWLED 2007), vol. 258 (2007)

9. Lee, C., Park, S., Lee, D., Lee, J., Jeong, O., Lee, S.: A comparison of ontology reasoning systems using query sequences. In: ICUIMC '08: Proceedings of the 2nd International Conference on Ubiquitous Information Management and Communication, pp. 543–546. ACM, New York, NY, USA (2008). http://doi.acm.org/10.1145/1352793.1352907

10. Motik, B., Sattler, U.: A comparison of reasoning techniques for querying large description logic ABoxes. In: Proceedings of the 13th International Conference on Logic for Programming, Artificial Intelligence and Reasoning (LPAR 2006), pp. 227–241 (2006)

11. Motik, B., Sattler, U.: Practical DL reasoning over large ABoxes with KAON2 (2006). Unpublished. Available at http://kaon2.semanticweb.org

12. Sirin, E., Parsia, B.: Pellet: An OWL DL reasoner. In: V. Haarslev, R. Möller (eds.) Description Logics, CEUR Workshop Proceedings, vol. 104. CEUR-WS.org (2004)

13. Viterbo, J., Endler, M., Sacramento, V.: Discovering services with restricted location scope in ubiquitous environments. In: Proceedings of the 5th International Workshop on Middleware for Pervasive and Ad-hoc Computing (MPAC '07), pp. 55–60 (2007)

14. Viterbo, J., Sacramento, V., Rocha, R., Baptista, G., Malcher, M., Endler, M.: A middleware architecture for context-aware and location-based mobile applications. In: Proceedings of 32nd Annual IEEE Software Engineering Workshop (SEW-32), IEEE Computer Society (2008)

15. Zombori, Z.: Efficient two-phase data reasoning for description logics. In: Bramer, M. (ed.) Artificial Intelligence in Theory and Practice, vol. 276, pp. 393–402. Springer, Boston (2008). 10.1007/978-0-387-09695-7

Chapter 8
Evaluation

Abstract In this chapter we describe how our implementation of the Decentralized Reasoning Service (DRS) was tested in respect to its functional behavior and its performance and discuss the results that were found.

Keywords Ambient Intelligence · Ubiquitous computing · Context-awareness · Rule-based reasoning · Decentralized reasoning · Cooperative reasoning

8.1 Testbed

In order to test the correct functioning and evaluate the performance of our implementation of DRS, we ran different batches of tests. To run the Ambient Decentralized Reasoning Service (DRS/A)—representing the ambient infrastructure—we used a desktop PC with a Core 2 Duo 2.40 GHz processor and Windows Vista operating system. To run the Device Decentralized Reasoning Service (DRS/D)—representing the mobile device—we used a notebook with an Atom 1.60 GHz processor Windows XP SP2 operating system. These computers were interconnected through an IEEE 802.11 wireless network with 54 Mbps data transfer rate. Depending on the purpose of each test, we used specific context data files—i.e., ontologies—created with specific features, as will be described later. In the next section we describe the functional tests performed to check if the service was operating as expected, i.e., meeting the previously identified design strategies. In Sect. 8.3, we discuss the tests we executed to measure the performance of the service.

8.2 Functional Test

A set of tests was performed to check if our implementation met the functional attributes of the design strategies identified in the specification of the decentralized reasoning service, as enumerated in Sect. 4.3.1. As this operation involved the simulation of the client applications subscribing the service and context changes happening

J. Viterbo and M. Endler, *Decentralized Reasoning in Ambient Intelligence*,
SpringerBriefs in Computer Science, DOI: 10.1007/978-1-4471-4168-6_8,
© The Author(s) 2012

Fig. 8.1 Architecture used for the functional test

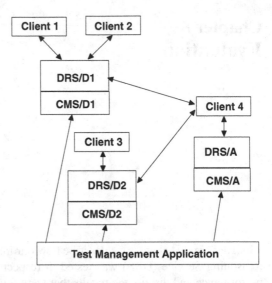

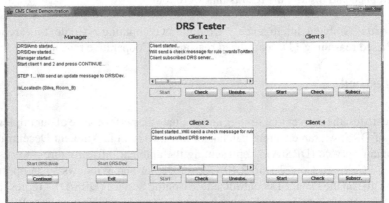

Fig. 8.2 GUI of the Test Management Application

in different sequences of events, we implemented a Test Management Application (TMA), with a graphical user interface to easily trigger the events and interpret the results. To be able to check any possible sequence of events, our simulation involved the execution of a reasoner service representing the ambient infrastructure (DRS/A), two reasoner services representing two users and their devices (DRS/D1 and DRS/D2), with the respective CMS servers, and four client applications, representing applications running on the users' devices (Client 1 and 2 running on device 1 and Client 3 running on device 2) and on the ambient infrastructure (Client 4). Figure 8.1 shows the architecture for this test.

The interface, shown in Fig. 8.2, contains buttons that allowed to control the actions of the TMA—responsible for simulating context changes for the reasoning services DRS/A, DRS/D1 and DRS/D2—and the four client applications, and windows to show the output of each application. For each entity, there is a start button. At left, a window shows messages describing the actions taken by TMA, which is responsible for sending context update messages to each CMS, triggering the inference of some rules provided by the clients. Each time the button "Continue" is pressed, TMA sends a message to a specific CMS, in a pre-defined sequence of steps. At right, four windows show the behavior of each client, i.e., the queries, subscriptions and notifications. There are also the buttons "Check", for sending a query, and "Subscribe/Unsubscribe", for posting or removing a subscription. Using this interface we could verify if the queries were answered correctly and if the notifications were triggered at the right moment and with the correct result. We tested these responses varying the order of events (subscriptions and notifications), the number the simultaneous subscriptions and the form of the interaction, testing all possible patterns (see Sect. 4.2). In each case the response was correct.

8.3 Performance Test

A second set of tests was conducted in order to verify the response time, communication traffic and memory consumption of our implementation, three of the non-functional attributes of the design strategies identified in the specification of service (Sect. 4.3.2). Usually AmI systems are represented by ontology context models where the ABox is very much larger than the TBox. In such cases, the use of KAON2, which was developed to efficiently reason over large ABoxes rather than large TBoxes [1], is more appropriate. Accordingly, to represent our system in the evaluation process, we created ontologies with this same feature, but with some other specific characteristics, only for purpose of performance testing.

For our performance test we tried to create an ontology representing a realistic scenario—based on our conference example—to observe the behavior of the DRS server under heavy use conditions that we tried to simulate. As described in Fig. 8.3, this ontology contains the four classes *Person*, *Activity*, *Subject* and *Environment* interrelated by the five binary properties *isLocatedIn*, *wantsToAttend*, *isInterestedIn*, *isRelatedWith* and *takesPlace*, and the unary property (subclass) *isAboutToStart*.

We generated a huge number of individuals and facts to create a large ABox, trying to mimic numbers that could possibly occur in a real scenario, e.g., a large conference. For example, in conference ACM SAC 2008, there were about 60 different sessions and the proceedings include approximately 1400 keywords. Based on these data, the ontology we generated has 500 individuals belonging to class *Person* ($Attendee_0$ to $Attendee_{499}$), 60 individuals belonging to class *Activity* ($Session_0$ to $Session_{59}$), 1400 individuals belonging to class *Subject* ($Keyword_0$ to $Keyword_{1399}$) and 10 individuals belonging to class *Environment* ($Room_0$ to $Room_9$). We then connected randomly each *Person* individual with one *Environment* individual (with *isLocatedIn* property), 10 *Activity* individuals (with *wantsToAttend* property) and 20 *Subject* individuals (with *isInterestedIn* property), each *Activity* individual with 30 *Subject*

Fig. 8.3 Classes and properties of the conference ontology

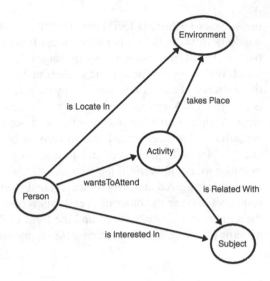

individual (with *isRelatedWith* property) and one *Environment* individual (with *takesPlace* property). No individual was defined as belonging to subclass *isAboutToStart*, for this was used to trigger the notification.

8.3.1 Response Time

In a first experiment, we measured the response time, i.e., the overall time since a context data change message is sent to the ambient side DRS, until an application client is notified by the user side DRS about the inference. We simulated the load of the server creating a variable number of subscriptions—100, 200, 300, 400 or 500—defined by a rule correlating the properties *wantsToAttend*, *takesPlace* and *isAboutToStart*, as in Rule 8.1.

Rule 8.1:

wantsToAttend("Attendee5", ?s) ∧ *takesPlace(?s, ?r)* ∧ *isAboutToStart(?s)* ⇒
shouldGoToRoom("Attendee5", ?r)

The purpose of this simulation was to observe the overhead caused by the monitoring process. Since our server is optimized to check (i.e., evaluate the rules) only the subscriptions that involve properties that are changed, we tested the server under two different conditions: under no context change and with a context change message (changing the *takesPlace* property of a individual from class *Activity* selected randomly) being sent to the remote reasoner at each 50 milliseconds.

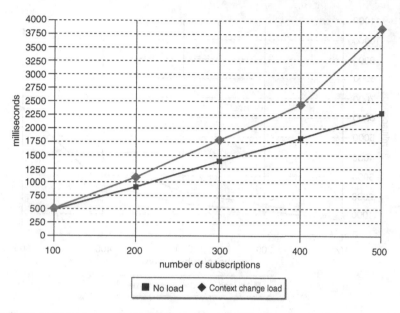

Fig. 8.4 Response time measured for DRS working in a centralized configuration

8.3.1.1 Centralized Reasoning

To be able to evaluate the decentralized reasoning strategy, we first measured the response time for a centralized configuration, i.e., with a central server collecting all context information and reasoning over a complete ontology, measuring the response time for the different number of subscriptions and load conditions. We created a test client that would subscribe the DRS with Rule 6.1 and then send a context change message that would trigger the context event. Hence, the total time observed goes from the sending of the context message until the receiving of the notification, encompassing the reasoning process.

Figure 8.4 shows the different values measured. We can easily notice the influence of a greater number of subscribers—with the time measured going approximately from 0.5 to 2.25s under no load—, due to time spent on notifying each subscriber when a rule holds. We can conclude also that the influence of the message load becomes bigger when the number of subscribers gets greater, observing that for 500 subscriptions the difference between the two experiments goes to about 1.5 s. That is due to the combination of the time spent monitoring and evaluating rules each time a message arrives with the time spent on notifying each subscriber.

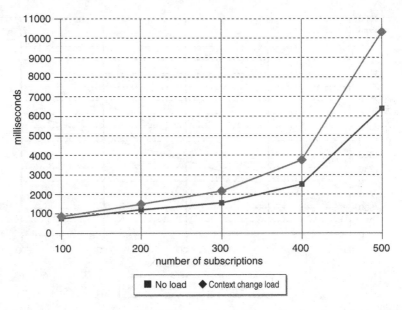

Fig. 8.5 Response time measured for DRS working in a decentralized configuration and the reasoning being triggered at the remote reasoner

8.3.1.2 Decentralized Reasoning Triggered at the Remote Reasoner

The decentralized reasoning was evaluated assuming a local reasoner (DRS/D) that would have the part of the ontology concerning a user and its device, having information about the binary properties *isLocatedIn*, *wantsToAttend* and *isInterestedIn* while the remote reasoner (DRS/A) would have the part of the ontology having data about the properties *isRelatedWith* and *takesPlace*, and the unary property (subclass) *isAboutToStart*. As the reasoner running on the user's device is not expected to operate under heavy load conditions, all the load was simulated at the DRS/A.

We first measured the response time with the notification event being triggered by a message received by the remote reasoner. For that purpose, we used a test client that would subscribe the local DRS with Rule 6.1—that would have part delegated to the remote reasoner—and then send a context change message to the remote reasoner that would trigger the context event. In this case, the total time observed goes from the sending of the context message to the remote reasoner until the receiving of the notification by the test client, encompassing also the reasoning process on the remote reasoner, the notification sent from the remote reasoner to the local reasoner and the validity verification of this notification by the local reasoner.

Figure 8.5 shows the two graphs. The influence of the number of subscribers is in even more perceptible in this configuration, making the measured time vary from approximately 0.8 s to 6.4 s under no load. This can be attributed to time spent by the remote reasoner to notify the simulated subscribers combined with the extra

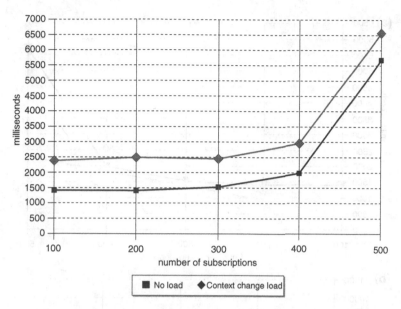

Fig. 8.6 Response time measured for DRS working in a decentralized configuration and the reasoning being triggered at the local reasoner

communication time. As observed in the centralized configuration, we notice that the influence of the message load becomes clearly bigger when the number of subscribers gets greater, observing that while for 100 subscriptions the difference between the two experiments is insignificant, for 500 subscriptions the value goes to approximately 3.7s. Again we believe that this is due to the combination of the time spent monitoring and evaluating rules each time a message arrives with the time spent on notifying each subscriber, added with the time spent in communication between the two reasoners.

8.3.1.3 Decentralized Reasoning Triggered at the Local Reasoner

Finally, we measured the response time with the notification event being triggered by a message received by the local reasoner (DRS/D). As in the previous configuration, only the remote reasoner (DRS/A) was subject to the load simulation. The test client used in this case would subscribe to the local DRS submitting Rule 6.1, which would be split and have part delegated to the remote reasoner. Then the test client would send to the local reasoner a context change message that would cause the sending of an update message to the remote reasoner, what would finally trigger the notification event. The total time measured for this configuration comprises everything observed in the previous configuration, plus the time needed for the reasoning process executed on the local reasoner and the time for the update message going from the local to the remote reasoner.

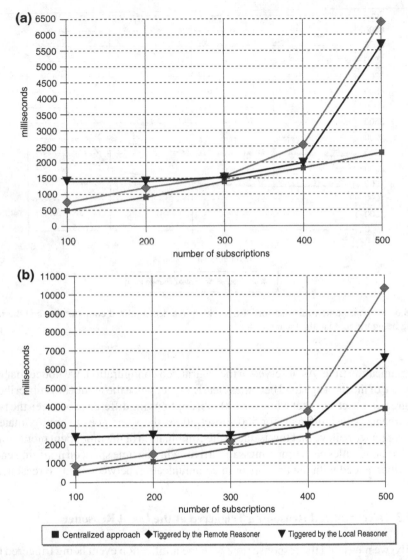

Fig. 8.7 Comparison of the three configurations **a** with no load and **b** with context change load

In Fig. 8.6, the two curves show the results for the experiments with and without load. In this graph we notice a peculiar behavior when comparing this configuration with the previously presented configuration. We can observe that the number of subscribers does have little impact until it becomes greater than 300. This is possibly due to the fact that most of the time of the reasoning operation is spent in communication among the reasoners.

8.3.1.4 Result Analysis

Figure 8.7 shows the response time measured for DRS with different load conditions in two different graphs, allowing the comparison of the performance of the three different configurations in each case. In Fig. 8.7a we see results found under no load and, in Fig. 8.7b the results with the simulation of the arrival of context change messages.

A behavior that becomes clear from both graphs is the fact that for a small number of subscriptions the response time tends to be greater for the decentralized reasoning triggered at the local reasoner. This fact can be explained by the greater overhead imposed by the extra communication starting at the local reasoner, compared with the relatively small amount of time necessary to process less subscriptions. On the other hand, we can observe that increasing the number of subscriptions influences the response time of the system more drastically for the decentralized reasoning triggered at the remote reasoner under a simulated load condition. In this configuration we find the worst case, which is about 10.5 s for 500 subscriptions. As, in this case, the remote reasoner is responsible for the *ambient side* reasoning, a context change will probably trigger several simultaneous notifications (to simulated subscribers), causing a high communication overhead.

8.3.2 Communication Traffic and Memory Footprint

In a second experiment, we compared DRS's decentralized reasoning approach both with a centralized and a simple peer-to-peer approach, all of them targeted at the evaluation of inference Rule 8.2, presented below, for the same ontology and test bed used in the first experiment.

Rule 8.2:

isLocatedIn("Silva",?r) $\wedge$ *takesPlace(?s,?r)* $\wedge$ *hasStarted(?s)* $\longrightarrow$ *isBusy("Silva")*

We measured the communication traffic between the mobile device and the network simulating different configurations. Distributed context providers were simulated by programs running in background and generating context change messages at each 5 seconds. To represent the mobile users, we implemented location providers, variating the *isLocatedIn* property. To represent the ambient context changes, we implemented activity status providers, indicating if a conference session *isAboutToStart*, *hasStarted* or *hasFinished*. While one location provider instance was executed on the netbook, all other context providers were deployed on the stationary machine.

For the decentralized reasoning approach, we set one location provider instance to send context change messages regarding the user's location to the user side DRS on the netbook, and the other location provider instances, together with the activity status provider instance, to send context change messages to the ambient side DRS.

Table 8.1 Communication overhead and memory footprint measured for different reasoning configurations simulated

	Centralized	Decentralized	Peer-to-peer
Communication traffic	790 Bytes/s	81.7 Bytes/s	303.5 KBytes/s
Memory footprint	—	20.2 KBytes	23.5 KBytes

For simulating and evaluating the centralized reasoning approach, a DRS server executing on the *ambient side* was set to be the sole reasoner, receiving all context change messages described previously. Since we could not find performance results of any related system implementing peer-to-peer reasoning approach, we decided to simulate a simple P2P system, where each *user side* DRS is responsible for performing all inferences locally using context updates received from all other peers (as in P2P-DR, discussed in Sect. 3.5). Thus, for setting up the P2P configuration, we executed the location provider representing the user on the netbook, and the additional 499 instances of location providers and the activity status provider were executed on the stationary machine, all configured to periodically broadcast context change messages to the user side DRS.

For these three approaches we measured the communication traffic at the netbook—accounting for both received and sent context change messages and the messages exchanged between the DRS services—during a simulation period of 5 minutes. We verified also the memory footprint of the reasoner executing on that device. From the measured values presented in Table 8.1, we observe that our decentralized approach minimizes the communication with the mobile device and, due to a smaller ontology, requires less memory at the user side.

8.4 Discussion

The response times observed in the first set of performance tests (Sect. 8.3.1) show that a some communication overhead is caused by the messages exchanged between the reasoners to perform the *cooperative reasoning*. In our simulation, the centralized reasoning showed a better performance in all cases, with a drastic difference for more than 300 subscribers. It is important to highlight, though, that in this configuration, the ambient's DRS and CMS would collect the context data of all sensors and mobile devices in the environment. In this experiment we did not take into account the huge communication overhead caused by periodic context data tranfer between the context providers and the ambient service in the centralized approach, as we were interested only in measuring the response time.

Thus, the results do not invalidate the use of the *cooperative reasoning process* in real scenarios. On the contrary, it proves its applicability, as in the worst case the response time was 10.5 s, which is acceptable for our target scenario with up to 500 devices. It means that a user could be notified about the imminent start of a conference session 10.5 s after it is signalled by the ambient infrastructure. Moreover, as discussed in Sect. 5.1.3, if the context change periodicity is not lesser than about 30 s—which is an acceptable value for our scenario, as we do not expect a user to change his location more frequently than that—the inference process would converge to a stable result.

Nevertheless, the increase in the slope of the graphs for more than 300 subscribes indicates that the present implementation is not scalable, i.e., it is not ready for use in scenarios where a huge number of clients request the reasoning service. We observe that the response time was greatly affected by the communication overhead when the number of subscriptions grew. On the other hand, the results observed in the second experiment (Sect. 8.3.2) showed that the communication traffic was much higher in the centralized configuration than in the *cooperative reasoning*. Besides that, the reasoning service in the cooperative approach presented a smaller memory footprint.

In the next section, we discuss the contributions and limitations of the proposed approach, presenting also some topics of future work.

Reference

1. Motik, B., Sattler, U.: Practical DL reasoning over large ABoxes with KAON2 (2006). Unpublished. Available at http://kaon2.semanticweb.org

Chapter 9
Conclusion

Abstract In this chapter, we recollect the main aspects of our work and draw our final remarks. In the next section, we present a brief review about this work, summarizing the most important issues we tackled. In Sect. 9.2, we discuss the importance of the proposed approach. Finally, in Sect. 9.3, we enumerate some ideas about future work.

Keywords Ambient Intelligence · Ubiquitous computing · Context-awareness · Rule-based reasoning · Decentralized reasoning · Cooperative reasoning

9.1 Summary

We proposed a decentralized reasoning approach for performing rule-based reasoning about context data targeting AmI systems, according to the characteristics of a specific model, where we assumed that there are two main interacting parties, the *user side* and the *ambient side*, and each side has access to different context information, which is not shared with the other side.

The provision of rule-based inference mechanisms is a fundamental requirement of middleware systems that aim at supporting the development and deployment of AmI services and applications. Rules provide a formal model for describing and detecting relevant situations for AmI applications. As such, using rules the application developer can define the relevant situations separated from the application code, achieving a higher degree of flexibility: he may easily modify existing rules to adapt applications to different domains or reuse available rules to describe new situations. Furthermore, the use of free variables in rules give even more flexibility in the description of situations, as the developer can refer generically to the elements of a domain, rather than mention them specifically.

The complexity of context reasoning in AmI systems is enhanced by the fact that applications, services, rules and context information may be partially or fully

J. Viterbo and M. Endler, *Decentralized Reasoning in Ambient Intelligence*,
SpringerBriefs in Computer Science, DOI: 10.1007/978-1-4471-4168-6_9,
© The Author(s) 2012

Table 9.1 Comparison of DRS with related work

	Type	Inference	Variables	Asynchronous
Gaia	Rule-based	Local	Yes	Yes
OWL-SF	Rule-based	Local	Yes	Yes
DRAGO	Classification	Distributed	No	No
P2P-DR	Rule-based	Distributed	No	No
P2PIS	Rule-based	Distributed	No	No
DRS	Rule-based	Two-tier	Yes	Yes

distributed among the different elements involved. Thus in some circumstances a centralized approach may be inefficient and even infeasible. In such environments, distributed reasoning is necessary to address the complexity that arises from the coexistence of different elements that collect, store, process, exchange and reason about context data. Approaches for distributed reasoning that try to overcome this limitation, such as Gaia [4], OWL-SF [3], DRAGO [5], P2P-DR [2] and P2PIS [1], provide solutions that either are not completely distributed, or are not capable of evaluating complex rules with variables, indicating that there must be a trade-off between these features.

As such, we proposed a simplified model for our system, where we assumed two main interacting parties in the reasoning process: the *user side* and the *ambient side*, both comprised by the services, applications and knowledge base that are available at each side, in a two-tier approach. In our model, not all context information is available both at the users' mobile devices and at the ambient infrastructure. Some information may be available only at the *user side*, while some other information may be available only at the *ambient side*.

Based on this model, we propose a strategy in which two entities—a reasoner running on the user side, the *device reasoner*, and another one running on the ambient side, the *ambient reasoner*—interact to infer situations described by rules involving context variables that refer to data collected at both sides, performing what we defined as *cooperative reasoning*. After identifying a set of general design strategies for implementing a distributed reasoning service tailored to the model we proposed, and formalizing the *cooperative reasoning* operation, we defined a complete process—comprising a protocol and the corresponding distributed algorithms—to execute the *cooperative reasoning*. Finally, we implemented the Decentralized Reasoning Service (DRS), a prototype middleware service for performing the *cooperative reasoning process*.

In Table 9.1, the main features of DRS are compared with those of the related systems discussed in Chap. 3. We can notice that—differently from DRAGO, P2P-DR and P2PIS—DRS is capable of executing rule-based reasoning using variables and providing asynchronous communications (pub/sub). And compared to Gaia and OWL-SF, DRS is capable of executing inference based on context data distributed in a two-tier scenario, i.e., involving the *user side* and the *ambient side*.

In the *cooperative reasoning process*, an important design strategy is to provide asynchronous communication (publish/subscribe). To achieve this goal in the *cooperative interaction*, a *local reasoner* has to constantly update the information forwarded to the *remote reasoner*. For that reason, if there are frequent context changes at the *local reasoner*, the reasoning operation may never converge. Besides that, the frequent update messages exchanged between the reasoners may cause a significant communication overhead, making this strategy inadequate for reasoning with highly variable context data.

One could be concerned if this data exchange between the *local reasoner* and the *remote reasoner* would compromise the user's privacy. However, as the *local reasoner* forwards no complete RDF tuple to the *remote reasoner*—but only tuples containing ontology individuals that represent specific values of context variables—there is not a complete knowledge sharing between those reasoners. As such, as far as the local part of the rule is not diclosed to the *remote reasoner*, the *local reasoner* is able to keep privacy about its context data.

Besides DRS, we implemented also the Context Model Service (CMS), a prototype service responsible for collecting context data from context providers available in a specific domain, keeping an updated representation of the assembled data according to a valid context model (an ontology), and providing access to up-to-date context information. Both CMS and DRS were implemented using the KAON2 reasoning API to access ontology data and perform reasoning operations. Since KAON2 was available only for J2SE environment, it was not possible to port our services also to mobile devices that execute only J2ME based applications. Moreover, to be used in real-world AmI scenarios, dealing with the dynamic and heterogeneous characteristics of such environments, these services must be executed on top of a more complex middleware architecture, capable of providing complementary functionalities such as service discovery or support to semantic interoperability.

DRS was submitted to a battery of tests. The functional tests indicated that the service worked as expected. In the performance tests we tried to compare the *cooperative reasoning* with a simulated centralized configuration. When measuring the response times for the cooperative approach, we got values that—in spite of being satisfactory—were greater than the values observed for the centralized approach. This result can be explained by the fact that in our simulation of the centralized configuration we did not account for the communication overhead caused by the interaction with a large number context providers. Corroborating this expectations, the measurements of the communication traffic showed that it was much higher in the centralized configuration than in the *cooperative reasoning*. Besides that, the reasoning service in the cooperative approach presented a smaller memory footprint.

Nevertheless, the present implementation is not scalable, i.e., is not ready for use in scenarios where a huge number of clients request the reasoning service. The scalability was hindered both by the increasing use of memory and communication overhead, when the number of subscriptions grows. In our tests, memory overflow limited by approximately 700 the number of subscriptions we could simulate, and for more than 300 subscriptions the performance was greatly affected.

9.2 Why Two-Tier?

There is a question that could easily come to the mind of the reader of this work. "Why adopting a two-tier approach instead of a multi-tier approach for modelling the AmI system?". In principle, the two-tier model is a novel approach that may be extended to fit a multi-tier model, as we discuss in the next section, but this entails several issues that were considered beyond the scope of this work. Moreover, the two-tier approach meets our initial goal of approaching the access to ambient services for the perspective of a single user, and not for multi-user ubiquitous applications.

There are other reasons for focusing only on user and ambient side reasoners, instead of investigating a generic multi-tier approach. Even if the ambient infrastructure contains several devices, it is not reasonable to have the inference of rules split among several devices. Instead, the inference should be performed on a central server, because (i) many of the available devices may have severe resource constraints and (ii) usually there is a stable network link interconnecting these devices. Besides, a multi-tier reasoning would have great impact on the stability and scalability of the system. The stability would be affected due to the need of having n parts of a rule simultaneously satisfied. Accounting for the communication latency between reasoners and the fact that some context values may change frequently, as we discussed in Sect. 5.1.3, a great number of *Update* messages (Steps S8 and S9 of our process, Sect. 5.1.2) would be necessarily exchaged among the n peers, having high impact on the stability of the system. As a consequence, also the scalability would be limited by the huge increase in the number of messages exchanged among the reasoners.

9.3 Future Work

We identify several topics that could be possibly tackled in future work. As a first issue, we think that the scalability of the DRS can be considerably improved. In our current prototype, we used the KAON2 API—which is relatively light, when compared to other available implementations—to implement the reasoning functionalities, but we did not try to optimize the use of memory, keeping large data structures (e.g., a Query object of the KAON2 API) stored in memory, as we focused on improving the execution time performance. However, in our tests we concluded that the time consumed with the reasoning operation was not critical, indicating that the implementation may be revised, prioritizing to reduce the use of memory.

The communication overhead is another factor that affects the scalability of our implementation, as it increases the response time when there is a great number of subscriptions. As such, the protocol may be improved to avoid the constant message exchange between the local an the remote reasoner. Instead of providing updates every time a single context variable changes, the update messages could be sent less frequently, aggregating changes on several context variables over a period of time. Of course this solution will affect the reasoning time of the system.

Some rules—or parts of rules—that are submitted to the reasoning service may be recurrent, i.e., the same or different applications may want to submit these same rules in several occasions. As such, providing persistence mechanisms for recurrent rules and their inferred results—for a specific AmI system and its applications—is a way of improving our service's performance. This mechanism could not only make a faster response time possible, but also extend the system's knowledge by creating a data base containing usual inference rules.

In fact, a thorough discussion about the service's expressiveness, which is currently bounded by the characteristics of the reasoning API, is still a task to be fulfilled. We intend to define the necessary conditions for the rules to be processed by the service to be DL-safe, so as to guarantee the decidability of the decentralized inference.

A direct way to improve our work is by making our protocol more robust so as to deal with communication problems, i.e., loss of messages, disconnections, etc. In our system model we assumed that the communication was reliable, i.e., there would be no loss of messages. As such, we did not include confirmation messages in our protocol, and hence, the loss of a message can cause an inference operation to be discontinued, with no warning being sent to the clients.

Another aspect to be approached in the future is to test our service using real world ubiquitous applications. Deploying our reasoner in such a real world scenario could bring great advantage, indicating problems to be corrected in our implementation or new functionalities to be added. The accomplishment of such task would enable a practical analysis of the non-functional attributes of the service, yielding their improvement and favouring a discussion about QoS aspects in AmI, which is still an open problem.

In our present work, the implemented service can not be executed in mobile devices with J2ME-compatible virtual machines, such as most smartphones and many PDA's. As the use of these devices is fundamental in ubiquitous systems, porting our implementation to this execution environment is a task with great priority.

In our scenario, privacy was mentioned as the main reason not to have all context information available in a central repository. However, in the present implementation of the cooperative DRS reasoner, even while the *local reasoner* keeps safely its local context data, other context information can be easily obtained from the *remote reasoner* as a result of some particular query. Hence, the addition of access control mechanisms to avoid the disclosure of specific information is a possible improvement to DRS.

Finally, it is important to give a new step towards a more general distributed reasoning scenario. Therefore, we intend to study how the proposed strategy could be extended to allow the inference of rules in scenarios where the context data is divided in more than two tiers.

References

1. Adjiman, P., Chatalic, P., Goasdoué, F., Rousset, M., Simon, L.: Distributed reasoning in a P2P setting: Application to the semantic web. J. Artif. Intell. Res. **25**, 269–314 (2006)
2. Bikakis, A., Antoniou, G.: Distributed reasoning with conflicts in an ambient peer-to-peer setting. In: Bergmann, R., Althoff, K.D., Furbach, U., Schmid, K. (eds.) Proceedings of the Workshop "Artificial Intelligence Methods for Ambient Intelligence" at the European Conference on Ambient, Intelligence (AmI'07), pp. 25–34 (2007)
3. Mrohs, B., Luther, M., Vaidya, R., Wagner, M., Steglich, S., Kellerer, W., Arbanowski, S.: OWL-SF—A distributed semantic service framework. In: Proceedings of Workshop on Context Awareness for Proactive Systems (CAPS), Helsinki, Finland, pp. 67–78 (2005)
4. Román, M., Hess, C., Cerqueira, R., Ranganathan, A., Campbell, R., Nahrstedt, K.: A middleware infrastructure for active spaces. IEEE Pervasive Comput. **1**(4), 74–83 (2002)
5. Serafini, L., Tamilin, A.: DRAGO: Distributed reasoning architecture for the semantic web. In: Gómez-Pérez, A., Euzenat, J. (eds.) ESWC, Lecture Notes in Computer Science, vol. 3532, pp. 361–376. Springer, Berlin (2005)